СН.

3 0147 0001 0423 5

DK290.3 .C44 A25 1984

Chernenko, K. U. (Konstantin
 Ustinovich), 1911-

Soviet-U.S. relations

SOVIET–U.S. RELATIONS

SOVIET-U.S. RELATIONS

The Selected Writings and Speeches of

Konstantin U. Chernenko

compiled and edited by

Victor Pribytkov

Published in cooperation with:
the Novosti Publishing House, Moscow

PRAEGER SPECIAL STUDIES • PRAEGER SCIENTIFIC

New York • Philadelphia • Eastbourne, UK
Toronto • Hong Kong • Tokyo • Sydney

Library of Congress Cataloging in Publication Data

Chernenko, K. U. (Konstantin Ustinovich), 1911-
   Soviet-U.S. relations.

   1.   United States- Foreign relations-Soviet Union-
3. Soviet Union-Foreign relations- 1975-   Addresses
essays, lectures. I. Pribytkov, V. (Victor), 1935-
II. Title.   III. Title: Soviet-US relations.
DK290.3.C44A25   1984   327.73047   84-23789
ISBN 0-03-003277-6 (alk. paper)

Published in 1984 by Praeger Publishers
CBS Educational and Professional Publishing
a Division of CBS Inc.
521 Fifth Avenue, New York, NY 10175 USA
© 1984 by Praeger Publishers

All rights reserved

456789 052 987654321

Printed in the United States of America
on acid-free paper

To The American Reader

Dear Reader,

I hope this book will in a certain measure help you better to understand how the Soviet Union sees the world, what it strives for, and what causes it supports. I think a collection of speeches and articles delivered and written at different times and on different occasions best serves this purpose. The material it contains reflects real moments of history in its onward movement and evaluates certain events as they occurred, not in retrospect.

I think you will notice that Soviet-American relations, in their different aspects, are dealt with in virtually every speech of mine. This is understandable, because our two countries bear a special responsibility for peace on earth, for making it possible for people in all countries to live and work in peace.

This is not a question of a subjective wish to shoulder or not to shoulder this responsibility. History, it may be said, has so decreed. Hence our attention and, I would add, carefully weighed approach to everything that determines relations between our countries, that may contribute to their improvement.

We find it hard to understand the reasoning of those who allege that tension in relations with the Soviet Union will inevitably be maintained, that it is almost predestined, and that the United States has nothing to lose by that.

There are also people in your country who assert that they are not against normal relations with the Soviet Union, that they are for talks with it and even for arms limitation agreements. But for this, they say, the United States must be

v

stronger than the Soviet Union. This, of course, is not so. Striving for military superiority and conducting honest businesslike talks on questions that affect the national security of the two parties are incompatible. The uncontrolled escalation of the arms race and its extension even to outer space—this, in the final analysis, is a threat to the United States' own security.

The attempts to achieve military superiority are fruitless and at the same time dangerous, and, of course, they cannot but complicate our relations. On the contrary, when both sides showed their readiness to adhere to the principles of equality and equal security and on this basis reached mutually acceptable accords, including agreements on arms limitation, the state of the relations between our countries changed for the better.

We have no alternative but to live together. This being so, it is better to live not in an atmosphere of enmity and fear, but in peace, as human beings should live, observing certain standards in our relations.

I hope that after familiarizing yourself with our country's approach to the issues of war and peace and of our specific proposals, you will be convinced that the Soviet Union is for equal and if possible, good relations with the United States, that it wants to reach agreement with the United States on a wide range of issues. We only want our proposals to be judged objectively, without prejudice. Prejudice and an unwillingness to recognize the truth have never done any good and today they may have the gravest consequences.

I wish the readers of this book in the United States prosperity and peace.

Contents

SOVIET–U.S. RELATIONS

Konstantin Chernenko at the Moscow Palace of Congresses in the Kremlin, April 22, 1981.

Biography of
Konstantin Ustinovich Chernenko

Konstantin Ustinovich Chernenko, General Secretary of the CPSU Central Committee and Chairman of the Presidium of the USSR Supreme Soviet, was born on September 24, 1911, in the village of Bolshaya Tes in Novoselovo District in Krasnoyarsk Territory (Eastern Siberia) into a family of Russian peasants. Konstantin Chernenko began his working life at an early age as a hired farm laborer.

Konstantin Chernenko's entire life has been devoted to work, first in Komsomol and later in Party bodies. In 1929 and 1930, as a young Komsomol member, he was in charge of the propaganda department of the Novoselovo District Komsomol Committee in Krasnoyarsk Territory. He volunteered for the Red Army in 1930 and joined the Communist Party the following year. He served with the border guards until 1933, and was elected secretary of a Party cell at a border post. Konstantin Chernenko reminisced:

> The years of my army service, difficult, anxious and exciting, are imprinted on my memory forever. I always remember them with sincere warmth and gratitude. It was in the Red Army that I was admitted to the Communist Party. This was one of the most important events in my life. Here the Communists among the border guards elected me Party organization secretary. Since then, my whole life has centered on Party work.

After completing his army service, Konstantin Chernenko worked in Krasnoyarsk Territory where he held different posts, head of the propaganda department of the Novoselovo

1

and Uyar District Party Committees, director of the Krasnoyarsk Territory House of Party Education, deputy head of the propaganda and agitation department and then Secretary of the Krasnoyarsk Territory Party Committee.

From 1943 to 1945 Konstantin Chernenko studied at the Higher School of Party Organizers under the Central Committee of the All-Union Communist Party (Bolshevik). On completing his studies he worked as Secretary of the Penza* Regional Party Committee. Three years later he was sent to the Moldavian Soviet Socialist Republic† where he was given the post of head of the propaganda department of the Central Committee of the Communist Party of Moldavia. In this post he devoted much of his strength and knowledge to economic and cultural construction in the Republic and to the communist education of the working people.

In 1956 Konstantin Chernenko was promoted to Central Committee of the Communist Party of the Soviet Union (CPSU) where he headed a sector at the propaganda department. In 1965 he was appointed head of the general department of the CPSU Central Committee. From 1966 to 1971 he was an Alternate Member of the CPSU Central Committee. At the Twenty-fourth Party Congress in March 1971 he was elected Member of the CPSU Central Committee and in March 1976, at the plenary meeting of the CPSU Central Committee held after the Twenty-fifth Party Congress, he was elected Secretary of the CPSU Central Committee. In 1977 he became an Alternate Member of the Political Bureau and in 1978 a Member of the Political Bureau of the CPSU Central Committee.

For many years now the Soviet people have elected Konstantin Chernenko to the highest body of state authority—the Supreme Soviet of the USSR.

At the extraordinary plenary meeting of the CPSU Central Committee in February 1984 Konstantin Chernenko was unanimously elected General Secretary of the CPSU Central Committee. On April 11, 1984, the first session of the USSR Supreme Soviet of the eleventh convocation elected him Chairman of the Presidium of the USSR Supreme Soviet.

---

* Penza is a city (current pop. 522,000) approx. 450 miles southeast of Moscow.

† Moldavia is a large industrial and agricultural republic located in the Western European part of the Soviet Union and is one of the 15 constituent Soviet Socialist Republics.

Konstantin Chernenko is well known as a talented organizer and an outstanding Party and state figure. While working in the Political Bureau and the Secretariat of the CPSU Central Committee, he put a great deal of effort into establishing and developing an effective and creative style of Party and state leadership involving a deep understanding of the key questions of social development and a realistic approach to assessing what has been achieved and what still remains to be done. Konstantin Chernenko is distinguished by his ability to inspire others with his energy and innovative attitude toward any problem, and to unite people for collective work.

Konstantin Chernenko is very interested in the life of the Soviet people and the way they think. He listens attentively to what they have to say. In recent years he has met with workers and employees at the Khromatron plant in Moscow, with workers in Tbilisi, Krasnoyarsk Territory, Chelyabinsk, and Frunze. At each meeting he has displayed a deep interest in their work, everyday problems, and opinions about the state of affairs in the country. Konstantin Chernenko stressed the importance of such meetings in his report at the June 1983 plenary meeting of the CPSU Central Committee:

> We should not turn away from frank discussions with people. We must be able not only to explain our policy and teach the people but also to learn from the people, one may say, to get charged with their strength. This should be not only a duty but also a need of every leading official. Political speeches and regular business reports to working people are the touchstone by which an official's ability to organize and draw the people behind him is judged. This was how Lenin saw it. That is how the Central Committee of our Party sees it.

The inexhaustible source of the Communist Party's strength lies in the deep, organic, and constantly growing links with the masses. These links and reliance on the masses form the basis of the entire activity of the CPSU Party and state apparatus. It is this idea that runs through Konstantin Chernenko's fundamental work, *Questions of the Party and State Apparatus,* published in 1982. The book states:

> We can say without any exaggeration that the most profound democracy lies at the heart of the Leninist style of leadership. It is conditioned by the very nature of the

Communist Party, by its aims and tasks, by its principles
of life and work. It is a style of leadership that implies
deep trust in the people and great responsibility to them;
it implies doing everything possible to promote the development of the creative activity of the working people; it
implies real humanism in all the activities of the CPSU and
the Soviet socialist state. A good knowledge of the mood,
concerns, and hopes of the Soviet people is the immutable
standard of Party and state leadership and supervision.

Konstantin Chernenko believes that a leader of our times
must be totally devoted to his work, have a broad knowledge
of it, be a talented organizer, be well-educated culturally,
have the ability to think sweepingly, feel the new and recognize
it in practice, and be intolerant of the least stagnation. This
type of leader must always rely on the Party committees, on
the Soviets of People's Deputies, which are truly mass bodies
of state authority, on the trade unions, the Komsomol, and
all public organizations.

Konstantin Chernenko has written a number of works
that comprehensively substantiate the growing role of the
CPSU in building a communist society. In the article entitled,
"The Leninist Strategy of Leadership," (*Communist,* no. 13,
1981), he stated that the growth of the Party's leadership role
under developed socialism is a reflection of the objective need
for socialist society's further progress at its mature stage, and
not the subjective desire of some individuals.

The realization of the great potential of developed socialism,
the transfer to intensification of the national economy, are
possible only on the basis of a thorough grasp of science,
including economic and social laws, and with the most
active, creative participation of the working masses. Only
the Party can draw up a scientifically based strategy to
promote the enthusiasm of the masses and direct it into
organized and planned work.

In his books, articles, and speeches Konstantin Chernenko refers to the works of Marx, Engels, and Lenin. A
heedful attitude towards their heritage and its creative application in modern conditions, in his opinion distinguishes a
true Marxist in our time. He stated in one of his speeches
that experience of revolutionary struggle and experience of
socialist and communist construction resolutely teach us to

oppose dogmatism, ossified ideas, and the heedless use of ready-made plans and stereotypes. As Lenin stressed, Marxism is not a dogma, but guidelines for action. So too is Leninism.

> The flow of life is swift. Problems that have been solved are replaced by new ones awaiting solution. That which was right yesterday may become wrong tomorrow. This means that we must notice, catch in time new phenomena and processes, analyze them and draw conclusions from them and give new theoretical orientations for their use in practice.*

Konstantin Chernenko has devoted much of his attention to strengthening the defense capability and security of the Soviet state and of its friends and allies. These efforts, he believes, are undertaken to strengthen worldwide peace and international security.

Konstantin Chernenko takes an active part in formulating the strategic directions of the peaceful foreign policy of the Soviet State. Specific emphasis is devoted to curtailing the race to build up nuclear and other arsenals and to preventing a nuclear war, and to promoting friendly cooperation between nations in all areas of human activity.

In 1975, Konstantin Chernenko went to Helsinki as a member of the Soviet delegation to the International Conference on Security and Cooperation in Europe. Commenting on the importance of this forum in his article, "Trust and Cooperation Among Peoples—A Guarantee of Peace and Security," (*International Affairs*, no. 9, 1980) he wrote:

> As a member of the Soviet delegation at the Conference in Helsinki, I feel particularly strongly the great positive impact of its decisions on the normalization of international relations, on the strengthening of mutual understanding, and on the spreading of the spirit of détente. During the past five years the peoples of the world saw for themselves that it is possible to achieve mutual accord and understanding between states with different systems on complex foreign-policy issues even in difficult conditions, that it is possible to lessen and even remove mutual suspicion

---

* From the report at the Commemorative Meeting in Moscow, on April 22, 1981, dedicated to the 111th anniversary of Lenin's birth.

through contacts and talks, to expand mutual trust by developing multifaceted cooperation, that it is possible to improve and considerably ease the situation in Europe, thus strengthening international security and peace in general.

Four years later, Konstantin Chernenko took part in the Vienna talks with President Carter that preceded the signing of the SALT-II Treaty. Speaking about the Soviet Union's traditional adherence to the ideals of peace and disarmament and its consistent peaceful course, Konstantin Chernenko recently stressed:

Continuity in foreign policy means first of all that we should do everything possible to avert a nuclear catastrophe. This means that we must work for a real change for the better in the present dangerous development of world events. This means that we must move along the road of equal cooperation among states based on the principles of peaceful coexistence. In this spirit we are prepared to act jointly with all political and public forces and with all governments which pursue the same aims.

Konstantin Chernenko's "six principles," the norms by which relations between the nuclear powers should be governed, were put forward in a speech at a meeting with voters in Moscow on March 2, 1984. They have been given worldwide publicity and are supported by the peaceloving forces around the world.

For great services to his country, Konstantin Ustinovich Chernenko was given the Lenin prize, was twice awarded the title of Hero of Socialist Labor, decorated with four Orders of Lenin, three Orders of the Red Banner of Labor, three gold medals of the Hammer and Sickle, and many other medals of the Soviet Union. Konstantin Chernenko also holds the highest awards of other socialist countries.

The Conference in Helsinki and International Security

The following is an excerpt from an article by Konstantin U. Chernenko published in the Soviet monthly journal International Affairs* *(No. 11, November 1975). The article sums up the results of the Helsinki Conference on Security and Cooperation in Europe, which on August 1, 1975 culminated in the signing of the Final Act of the conference by leaders of 33 states of Europe along with leaders of the U.S. and Canada. Konstantin U. Chernenko was a member of the Soviet delegation which participated in the final stage of the conference.*

Since the 1960s the Soviet Union and other countries of the socialist community have put forward a number of proposals on ensuring collective security in Europe. Of tremendous importance for this were the decisions of the Twenty-third Congress of the CPSU providing for measures to improve the situation and strengthen security in Europe.

In the Report of the CPSU Central Committee to the Twenty-third Party Congress Leonid Brezhnev emphasized that during the years that had elapsed since the Twenty-

* The journal was founded in August 1954 by the Znanie (Knowledge) Society. It has been printed in Russian and English since 1955 and has had a French edition since 1961. It covers a wide range of topics: international relations, the ideological struggle, the national liberation movement, life in socialist and capitalist countries. It carries commentaries, memoirs, texts of international documents with explanations, book reviews, etc. Among the contributors to *International Affairs* are prominent Soviet and foreign observers, political analysts, diplomats, statesmen, and public figures. The journal receives many letters from Soviet and foreign readers.

second CPSU Congress the Soviet Union, alongside other socialist countries, "has pursued a policy aimed at relaxing tension, strengthening peace, achieving peaceful coexistence of states with different social systems, and creating conditions in international life under which each nation would freely advance along the road of national and social progress." The Report noted the urgent need for the normalization of relations in Europe. Leonid Brezhnev said: "The Soviet Union is consistently advocating the strengthening of European security and peaceful, mutually advantageous cooperation among all European states." Taking in account that in this respect the development of businesslike ties is of great importance, the guidelines of the Twenty-third CPSU Congress charted a course of further extending foreign economic ties with socialist and developing countries, as well as with industrialized capitalist states displaying readiness to develop trade with the Soviet Union.

The policy of the CPSU, aimed at strengthening security in the European continent, has been clearly and convincingly expressed in Soviet proposals on military détente reduction of armaments; promotion of businesslike contacts; the convocation, with this aim in view, of an international conference; and also the achievement of a solution to the German issue, proceeding from the realities that have taken shape. This program provided a foundation for greater efforts on the part of the Soviet Union and the fraternal socialist countries in the struggle to ensure peace and security in Europe.

The Meeting of the Political Consultative Committee of the Warsaw Treaty countries, held in Bucharest in 1966, was a major milestone on that road. In the "Declaration on Strengthening Peace and Security in Europe" adopted by this meeting the member countries ardently appealed to all governments and nations, all forces of peace and progress in Europe, regardless of their ideological, political, or religious convictions, "to join efforts so that Europe—a major center of world civilization—may become a continent of all-round and fruitful cooperation between equal nations and a powerful factor of stability, peace, and mutual understanding throughout the world." The participants in the meeting pointed out that socialist countries had always consistently opposed the division of the world into military blocs or alliances, and stated that the Warsaw Treaty would be annulled if the North Atlantic alliance was dissolved. At the same time, it was emphasized that as long as the North Atlantic pact existed and aggressive imperialist forces threatened peace, the socialist countries were fully determined to strengthen their might and defense capability.

In developing these basic propositions, the declaration mapped out a concrete program of strengthening peace and security in the European continent. In particular, it envisaged the convocation of an all-European conference to discuss problems of European security and cooperation. The program, advanced by the socialist countries, opened up real prospects for establishing relations of peace and mutually beneficial cooperation among European states.

This program was supported by the Conference of 24 Communist and Workers' Parties of Europe, held in April 1967 in Karlovy Vary, which discussed problems of security.

In late February and early March 1968 a consultative meeting attended by delegates of 67 Communist and Workers' Parties was held in Budapest. The participants in the meeting expressed their support for the convocation of a new international meeting of Communist and Workers' Parties, and for consolidation of peace and international security.

In its work for European security, the Soviet Union, despite the intrigues of the aggressive forces, proceeded from the fact that there existed real prerequisites for achieving this aim. These included the growing influence of the socialist countries on world politics, invigoration of the struggle waged by communists and the general public for peace, the growing awareness of bourgeois politicians of the dangers involved in the arms race, and their enhanced interest in developing business relations.

The principled and consistent stand of the CPSU and the fraternal Communist and Workers' Parties was expounded at the International Meeting of Communist and Workers' Parties held in Moscow in June 1969. The document adopted at the meeting emphasized that "attainment of lasting security in this continent is a problem which holds a paramount place in the minds and aspirations of the European peoples."

It is important to note that the proposal to convene a European conference on security, which was advanced for the first time at the Bucharest meeting, won broad support. Since then the Warsaw Treaty states had turned their unremitting attention to questions of preparing and convening an all-European conference, in particular, to its composition and agenda. These issues were discussed at the meeting of the Political Consultative Committee in Budapest in March 1969; at the summit meeting of the socialist countries in Moscow in December 1969; and at the meetings of foreign ministers of the Warsaw Treaty states held in recent years.

In March 1969 the Political Consultative Committee of the Warsaw Treaty states called on all European countries to hold a preliminary meeting of representatives to agree on the procedure of the convocation of the conference and its agenda.

As subsequent developments have shown, the efforts of socialist countries to convene a conference on security and cooperation in Europe with the purpose of achieving a relaxation of tension were not in vain. Their initiative and persistency contributed to putting into practice the idea of collective security in Europe. On May 5, 1969, the government of Finland declared that it was ready to sponsor the conference and a preliminary meeting for its preparation, provided the governments concerned deemed it expedient. In supporting Finland's initiative, the Warsaw Treaty members at the sessions of their foreign ministers in 1969 and 1970 proposed to put on the agenda of the conference the questions of ensuring European security and renouncing the use of force in relations among European states; of extending trade, economic, scientific, and technical ties and cultural and political cooperation among European states; as well as of setting up a body on security and cooperation in Europe. These ideas met with opposition on the part of certain reactionary quarters in Western states.

At the Berlin Meeting of the Political Consultative Committee of the Warsaw Treaty states its participants issued, on December 2, 1970 a statement on questions of strengthening security and developing peaceful cooperation in Europe, in which they noted that the opponents of détente had not given up their dangerous activities. The participants in the Berlin meeting expressed the firm determination of the parties and governments of their respective countries to continue to work together for security in Europe. They laid special emphasis on the fact that the German Democratic Republic, and states which had not yet done so, for example the Federal Republic of Germany, should establish equitable relations as a necessary condition for ensuring lasting peace in Europe.

In February 1971, at their meeting in Bucharest, foreign ministers of the Warsaw Treaty states spoke in favor of going over to a "new and more active stage of preparing an all-European conference."

The signing of a series of bilateral agreements and treaties in the early 1970s, which began with the treaty between the Soviet Union and the Federal Republic of Germany, were major steps on the path toward improving relations between states with different social and political systems. The Treaty between the USSR and the Federal Republic of Germany, signed in Moscow on August 12, 1970, (its five-year anniversary was recently marked) is a reliable foundation for the development of relations between these two countries having different social systems. The development of these relations was accompanied by growing cooperation between the two countries, which has contributed to the achievement of European security.

The Twenty-fourth Congress of the CPSU devoted a great deal of attention to the situation in Europe. The Report of the CPSU Central Committee stressed that the preparations for an all-European conference had been switched to the plane of practical policy. It was pointed out that the following prerequisites were necessary to ensure security in Europe: the entry into force of the treaties signed by the USSR and by Poland with the Federal Republic of Germany; the solution of problems connected with West Berlin on the basis of respect for allied agreements and the sovereign rights of the German Democratic Republic; the establishment of equitable relations between the German Democratic Republic and the Federal Republic of Germany, based on generally accepted norms of international law, and also the admission of these two states to the UN; the meeting of Czechoslovakia's just demand that the Munich deal of 1938 be declared null and void from the very beginning.

The Resolution adopted by the Twenty-fourth Congress of the CPSU noted that ensuring European security on the basis of recognizing the territorial and political realities that had emerged as a result of the Second World War was a key problem of strengthening universal peace and détente. Further development and deepening of relations between the USSR and France, the Resolution went on, was of great importance.

The signing in 1970 of the treaty between the USSR and the Federal Republic of Germany, and the Treaty between the Polish People's Republic and the Federal Republic of Germany, the ratification of which will promote an improvement of the situation in Europe, were important steps toward ensuring security in our continent. "A conference on security and cooperation in Europe should contribute to a further improvement of the European situation."

It is stressed in the Peace Program, worked out at the Twenty-fourth CPSU Congress, that in solving European problems one should proceed from a final recognition of the territorial changes in Europe that had taken place as a result of the Second World War; make a radical turn toward détente and peace in Europe; convene and successfully complete an all-European conference; and do everything to ensure collective security in Europe.

The Soviet Union reaffirmed the readiness jointly expressed by the Warsaw Treaty states to agree to the simultaneous dissolution of the Warsaw Treaty Organization and the North Atlantic organizations. . . .

In implementing the decisions of the Twenty-fourth CPSU Congress, Soviet diplomacy has taken a number of important steps which are of fundamental importance for the strengthening of European security. The Quadripartite Agreement on West Berlin, signed by the Soviet Union, the U.S., Britain, and France on September 3, 1971, is a valuable contribution to the creation of a system of European security. The Agreement removed a dangerous seat of tension and friction between states in the heart of Europe and rebuffed the forces which for many years had been seeking to use West Berlin for subversive activities against the countries of the socialist community. . . .

The signing on December 21, 1972, of the Treaty on the Principles of Relations between the German Democratic Republic and the Federal Republic of Germany was a new step toward eliminating the vestiges of the cold war in Europe. The Treaty stresses that the parties to it "are developing normal goodneighborly relations between them on the basis of equality" and observance of the UN Charter. They "shall resolve their disputes exclusively by peaceful means" and "shall refrain from the threat or use of force." The Treaty confirmed the "inviolability of the borders between them now and in the future." It also emphasized that "neither of the two states can represent the other one in international affairs or act on its behalf,'' and that the sovereign power of each of the two is confined to its state territory.

In conformity with the understanding reached, a treaty on mutual relations between Czechoslovakia and the Federal Republic of Germany was signed in Prague on December 11, 1973. It states that the Munich deal of 1938 was imposed on Czechoslovakia by the Nazi regime under the threat of force and the parties regard it as null and void. At the same time, Czechoslovakia and the Federal Republic of Germany pledged to resolve disputes exclusively by peaceful means and refrain from the threat or use of force. They reaffirmed the inviolability of their common borders now and in future and declared that they had no territorial claims on each other and would not make them in the future. The treaty also provides for an extension of economic, scientific, and technological cooperation. In late 1973 an agreement was reached under which Hungary and Bulgaria established diplomatic relations with the Federal Republic of Germany.

Signed and ratified, the treaties of the USSR, Poland, the German Democratic Republic, and Czechoslovakia with the Federal Republic of Germany, like the agreement on West Berlin, have made up a definite system of treaties which have opened up the path toward creating a new structure of relations between states with different social systems in Europe, and toward ensuring durable European security. These documents reflected the growing role of the socialist community in world affairs, the constructive policy of which has become an important factor in consolidating European security and universal peace.

The Declaration of Peace, Security, and Cooperation in Europe, adopted by the Political Consultative Committee of the Warsaw Treaty states at its meeting in Prague in January 1972, was a new step in the struggle to resolve European issues. The USSR and fraternal socialist countries came out in favor of recognizing and implementing the following basic principles of security and relations between European states: inviolability of borders, including those which emerged as a result of the Second World War; nonuse of force and solution of all disputes exclusively by peaceful means; peaceful coexistence of European states belonging to different social systems; good-neighborly relations and cooperation in the interests of peace; mutually advantageous ties between countries in economic, scientific, technical, and cultural fields, in the sphere of tourism and environmental protection; disarmament; and support for the United Nations.

As time passed, these principles evoked broad response from the public and many governments of European countries, and contributed to mutual understanding as far as the preparations for an all-European conference were concerned.

In December 1971 foreign ministers of the Warsaw Treaty states examined the problem of preparing the convocation of an all-European conference and confirmed the consent of their respective governments to Finland's proposal to hold multilateral consultations of the countries concerned in order to reach agreement on the agenda, working procedures, and dates and order of convening the conference.

These consultations were held in Helsinki from November 22, 1972 to June 8, 1973. They became possible as a result of essential changes in international relations which are marked by growing striving for negotiations between all states, big and small.

During the consultations, representatives of the Soviet Union and other socialist states contributed to the establishment and preservation of a businesslike atmosphere, displayed flexibility and made constructive proposals. The difficulties that emerged due to the different stands taken by the participants in the consultations, and also the urge of some Western circles to wreck an all-European conference, were gradually overcome. The fact that security and cooperation in Europe are equally in the interests of all European states has, in the final analysis, facilitated reaching an agreement on the inclusion in the agenda of the Conference on Security and Cooperation in Europe* of the following items recorded in the

---

* The Conference on Security and Cooperation in Europe, with the participation of 33 European countries, the United States, and Canada was convened on the initiative of the socialist countries. Consultative meetings were held prior to the regular Conference from November 1972 to June 1973. The first stage of the Conference, involving the 33 European foreign ministers, was held in Helsinki on July 3–7, 1973. The second stage of the Conference, with all 35 states participating, was held from September 18, 1973 to July 21, 1975 in Geneva. The third stage, involving political and state leaders from the 35 participating countries, was held from July 30 to August 1, 1975 in Helsinki, when the Final Act was signed and became an important factor ensuring peace in Europe.

The Conference was a milestone on the road to consolidating principles of peaceful coexistence and improving relations on the basis of equal cooperation among states with different social systems.

"Final Recommendations of the Consultations in Helsinki":

> questions pertaining to security in Europe;
> cooperation in economy, science, technology, and nature con-
> servation;
> cooperation in the humanitarian and other spheres;
> steps to be taken after the Conference.

It was decided to hold a conference in three stages. The first stage was held in Helsinki in the summer of 1973 and was attended by foreign ministers. The second stage of the Conference was held in Geneva and was a unique phenomenon in world politics. For almost two years, representatives of 33 states of Europe, and of the U.S. and Canada drafted concerted solutions. The second stage was completed in July 1975.

Of expecially great importance was the third, concluding stage of the Conference. The Soviet Union and other socialist countries proposed that it be held at the summit level. . . .

Helsinki served as the venue of the third stage which on August 1, 1975, culminated in the signing of the Final Act of the Conference† by the leaders of 35 states.

The world public, statesmen, and political figures thought highly of the successful convocation of the Conference in Helsinki and considered it an epoch-making achievement of progressive forces, furnishing favorable conditions for a fur-ther development of international relations. . . . *Rudé Právo* wrote: "It is gratifying that not only in the socialist countries which put forward the idea of convening the Conference but also among the realistically-minded circles in capitalist states the view prevails that the Final Act signed in Helsinki constitutes a reliable foundation for further unilateral, bilateral and multilateral efforts of the participating countries for years and even decades ahead."

People both in the East and in the West of our continent justly regard the decisions adopted by the Conference as a guarantee for a lasting peace. The view of Michel Debres, a prominent member of the Gaullist Party and former French defense minister, is indicative in this respect. Recently he wrote in *Figaro:*

---

† The Final Act stipulates that periodic conferences of the represen-tatives of the states participating in the Helsinki Conference be held to verify how the recommendations of the Final Act are being implemented. The first follow-up meeting took place in Belgrade from October 1977 to March 1978; the second in Madrid from November 1980 to September 1983.

It is self-evident that a French political leader and many others together with him should find in the Helsinki Conference a subject for contemplation—what stand should our country take not only in the coming months but also in the coming years? It is necessary above all to realize our urgent need for security, to be more exact, for détente. This is what the whole of Europe needs, and for us, in particular, it is imperative. . . . Whether one wishes it or not, for a period of time which cannot be specified détente is tied up with the preservation of the territorial borders established after the Second World War.

The significance of the Conference for consolidating peace and security in Europe and elsewhere is reflected in the work of the Thirtieth Session of the UN General Assembly which has opened in New York. In their speeches heads of many delegations pointed to the historic importance of consolidating the principles of peaceful coexistence as standards of relations between states with different social systems.

* * *

The Soviet Union and other socialist countries intend to abide strictly by the commitments which follow from the Final Act. The Soviet Union believes that all the other states, too, will strictly implement the accords achieved.

Speaking in Helsinki, Leonid Brezhnev, head of the Soviet delegation, emphasized that the overall result of the Conference was that "international détente is becoming increasingly filled with concrete material content. It is realization of détente that is the heart of the matter, the essence of what should make peace in Europe genuinely solid and unshakeable."

The document, On the Results of the Conference on Security and Cooperation in Europe, adopted by the Political Bureau of the CPSU Central Committee, the Presidium of the USSR Supreme Soviet, and the USSR Council of Ministers contains a clear-cut definition of the ways of implementing détente. The document reads in part: "The most important thing now is to complement political détente with military détente."

Reduction and then discontinuation of the arms race, and advancement toward universal and complete disarmament, are the supreme needs of the time. As is known, the Soviet

Union has long been speaking out in favor of the convocation of a World Disarmament Conference in order to approach a cardinal solution of this vital issue of world politics. As far as the prospects for a cessation of the arms race are concerned, the world public has welcomed a number of measures taken in recent years by the USSR and the U.S. aimed at averting a nuclear missile war, primarily, the measures to limit strategic weapons. New achievements in this direction would, undoubtedly, make a major contribution to the realization of détente, and would be totally in the interest of Europe.

Of late the attention of the public has been drawn to the work of a UN ad hoc committee for the World Disarmament Conference. As was seen from the speeches of delegates from many states, the Soviet initiative to convene such a conference is supported by the majority of UN members. Its convocation will facilitate the solution of a major task of our day. The Soviet proposal to include in the agenda of the Thirtieth session of the UN General Assembly the question of the signing of a treaty on complete and universal prohibition of nuclear weapon tests serves the same purpose.

To make détente a reality, large-scale comprehensive work in the sphere of economic cooperation among states has to be carried out. This sphere has not only a commercial significance, because trade and economic ties providing opportunities for commodity exchange at the same time strengthen the political foundation underlying relations among states, making them interested in the steady development of mutual relations.

Experience shows that cooperation in economy, industry, science, technology, and environmental protection can develop on the basis of equality and in accordance with the mutual interests of the partners. The agreements between the USSR and France, the Federal Republic of Germany, Italy, and Great Britain, as well as the agreements of Western countries with other socialist states, which are being successfully implemented, are a case in point. These agreements envisage not only elementary forms of economic exchange (mutual trade) but also the putting into effect of a number of joint large scale projects, including those on a compensation basis.

Experience also shows that there are broad opportunities for multilateral and bilateral cooperation in Europe. It is conceivable to carry out projects of common interest to the whole of Europe on a bilateral basis; for example, projects of electric power exchange to achieve a more rational use of the capacities of European power stations; cooperation in finding new sources of energy, including the development of atomic energy; building roads, creating a single navigation system in Europe; and so on. The present-day economic potential and natural resources of European countries, both socialist and capitalist, make their long-term cooperation possible in the above-mentioned and other spheres if they pool their efforts in carrying out large-scale projects. The bilateral agreements which have already been signed between socialist and capitalist countries have, in fact, laid the foundations for multilateral all-European cooperation. One of the tasks of translating détente into reality consists in removing all the barriers still left in its path.

The Leninist Strategy of Peace
in Action

The following is an excerpt from an article by Konstantin U. Chernenko containing a scientific analysis of the guidelines of Soviet foreign policy put forward by the Twenty-fifth Congress of the Communist Party of the Soviet Union. The article appeared in the Soviet monthly journal International Affairs *(No. 4, April 1976).*

The decisions of the Twenty-fifth Congress of the CPSU, which further mapped out the major steps in the socioeconomic development of the Soviet Union and impressive prospects for the creative work of the Soviet people, attract the attention of broad sections of the public the world over and inspire the progressive forces everywhere in their struggle for peace, democracy, and social progress.

The Congress of Soviet Communists once again showed to the whole world the purposefulness and consistency of the home and foreign policy pursued by the Party of Lenin, which sees its mission in serving the broadest masses of the working people, founds its work on the immortal teaching of Marxism-Leninism, and confidently puts its great ideals into life. The Twenty-fifth CPSU Congress gave further striking evidence that the Party's home and foreign policies are fused into a single whole and that the peaceful creative work of the Soviet people and the implementation of the grandiose plans for the building of communism are fully consonant with the Soviet Union's foreign policy of peace, which is aimed at consolidating peace and friendship among nations, supporting all progressive and peace-loving forces, and repulsing the forces of reaction and war. In its turn, the success achieved through this policy is inseparable from the Soviet Union's socioeconomic progress, from the strengthening of its economic, material, and technical potential, from the growth of its might, and from the rise of the Soviet people's living standard. . . .

In the period between the Twenty-fourth and Twenty-fifth Congresses the Soviet Union, led by the Leninist Party, made considerable headway in all spheres of building Communism. The fulfillment of the Ninth Five-Year Plan assignments made it possible to bring the socialist economy to a qualitatively new level and to achieve signal success in building the material and technical basis of communism and raising the people's standard of living. The Report of the Central Committee delivered by the General Secretary of the CPSU Central Committee, Leonid Brezhnev, and the Report on the Guidelines for the Development of the National Economy of the USSR for 1976–1980 delivered by the Chairman of the Council of Ministers of the USSR, Alexei Kosygin, gave an arresting picture of the Soviet people's remarkable achievements in their drive to expand production and comprehensively develop the national economy. The data cited in these reports spotlight the might of the Soviet economy which, being free of declines and crises, develops dynamically and by plan in the interests of the whole of society and the entire nation.

Under the Ninth Five-Year Plan, the growth rate of industrial output, capital investments, and allocations for new steps to raise the living standard was higher than in any preceding five-year period. During the last five years the fixed production assets increased by 50 percent, the national income rose by 28 percent, and real per capita incomes by 24 percent, and there was an increment of 43 percent in the volume of industrial output.

While the capitalist countries are suffering from a deepening crisis, the Soviet economy is steadily developing: production has reached a colossal scale in the Soviet Union, which today occupies first place in the world for the output of many vital products such as oil, steel, coal, iron ore, cement, and mineral fertilizers.

On the basis of the results achieved in promoting the nation's productive forces, and of socialism's immense creative potentialities, the CPSU Congress has set imposing objectives that inspire the Soviet people to move to new achievements in their work. In the Guidelines for the Development of the National Economy of the USSR for 1976–1980, adopted by the Congress, provisions are made for increasing the fixed production assets by 40 percent, industrial output by 35–39 percent, and the annual average agricultural output by 14–17 percent. These figures spell out a steady growth of the country's wealth and improvement of the Soviet people's well-being. Real per capita incomes are to increase by 20–22 percent.

The developed socialist society built in the USSR is demonstrating its huge potentialities, its ability to expand the productive forces rapidly, and, on that basis, improve the life of the people and carry out major social tasks.

The results of and prospects for socioeconomic development in the other countries of the socialist community likewise show a rapid growth of the productive forces and steady progress in all areas of life. During the past five years, industrial growth in the CMEA* states was four times faster than in the industrialized capitalist countries. A further considerable economic and social progress is envisaged for the coming five years in all the countries of the world socialist community. Againt the background of the economic, monetary, and sociopolitical upheavals afflicting the capitalist world, real socialism is vividly demonstrating its advantages over the bourgeois system. The fulfillment of the plans adopted by the socialist countries and the attainment of the objectives set in the program for socialist economic integration will be

---

* The Council for Mutual Economic Assistance is an interstate organization of socialist countries set up in 1949. By pooling and coordinating efforts the CMEA contributes to improving cooperation, planning the development of the economies, speeding scientific and technological advance, and raising the level of industrialization in those countries where industry is less developed, increasing industrial productivity, closing the gap of economic disparity, and raising the standard of living. Its member states are Bulgaria, Czechoslovakia, Cuba, Hungary, the German Democratic Republic, Mongolia, Poland, Rumania, the Soviet Union, and Vietnam, with Yugoslavia participating in the work of several Council bodies while the Democratic People's Republic of Korea, Laos, Angola, and Ethiopia have observer status. The CMEA cooperates with Finland, Iraq, and Mexico, as well as with 60 international organizations, on the basis of special agreements.

an important milestone in the drive to strengthen socialism's international positions and achieve new success in the economic competition with capitalism.

There are few skeptics in the world today who doubt the attainability of the targets set by the socialist countries. What is a plan assignment today will become a reality in the everyday life of millions of people tomorrow. The profound scientific substantiation of the policy worked out by the Communist parties, which are at the helm of power in the socialist countries, has been borne out by practice, by the experience of building socialism and communism, by the entire course of historical development.

Soviet people are confident that the plans adopted by the twenty-fifth Congress, as had been the case with the decisions of previous Congresses, will be consistently carried out; that through the work of the Party and the entire nation they will be translated into tangible material and cultural progress. They enthusiastically support the line adopted by the twenty-fifth Congress and this support is the powerful source of the efficacy of the Party's policy and of its transformative power.

A specific of the work of the CPSU is that its home and foreign policies represent an integral whole; they are closely linked, mutually conditioned, and directed toward the attainment of common aims. In its internal policy the Communist Party is working to carry out the program slogan of "everything for the sake of man, for the benefit of man." This is the principal aim of the Tenth Five-Year Plan, which consists of a steady rise of the people's living standard and cultural level through the dynamic and balanced development of social production and an enhancement of its efficiency; accelerated scientific and technological progress; higher labor productivity; and the utmost improvement of the quality of work in all sectors of the national economy. In order to ensure the most favorable external conditions for the successful attainment of this goal, the CPSU is consistently and perseveringly pursuing a policy of strengthening peace and international security and promoting friendly cooperation between nations and peaceful coexistence with capitalist countries.

By unswervingly pursuing this line the CPSU demonstrates the unbreakable continuity of its policy and fidelity to Leninist principles and traditions. Ever since the Soviet state was established, the building of a new society and the safeguarding of peace have been regarded as links of one chain. In the attainment of these aims the Soviet state's internal and external policies have always complemented each other. As early as 1919, when the Civil War was nearing its end, Lenin said at the Seventh All-Russia Congress of Soviets: "[A]head of us lies the main period of peaceful construction which means so much to all of us, which we desire, which we must carry out and to which we shall dedicate all our energies and our whole lives." In the same speech he repeated the Soviet Government's peace proposals to the Entente,* declaring that the "Russian Socialist Federative Soviet Republic wishes to live in peace with all peoples and devote all its efforts to internal development."

The resolution proposed by Lenin and passed by the Congress of Soviets† instructed the All-Russia Central Executive Committee,‡ the Council of People's Commissars,** and the People's Commissariat for Foreign Affairs*** "to continue this peace policy systematically, taking all appropriate measures to ensure its success."

Strictly in keeping with Lenin's behests, the CPSU orients its foreign policy on ensuring a lasting world peace and security, on ruling out wars from the life of human society. . . .

The impressive results of the efforts of the CPSU and the entire Soviet people to carry out the Peace Program and to achieve the foreign policy aims set by it, were given full expression in the Central Committee's Report to the Twenty-fifth Congress and in the speeches of the delegates and guests of the Congress.

"This program," Leonid Brezhnev said in his Report, "showed the realistic way to end the cold war and set clear objectives in the struggle to replace the danger of wars with peaceful cooperation."

Under the powerful impact of socialist foreign policy, far-reaching changes have taken place in the world, the

---

* Refers to the alliance of over 20 states, including the United States, France, Great Britain, Japan, etc., which organized an intervention against the young Soviet Republic in 1918–1920. The attempted invasion failed.

† Corresponding to the present-day session of the USSR Supreme Soviet (the Soviet legislature)

‡ Corresponding to the present-day Council of Ministers of the USSR (the executive body of power)

** Corresponding to the present-day Presidium of the USSR Supreme Soviet

*** Corresponding to the present-day USSR Ministry of Foreign Affairs

international climate has improved considerably, and a turn has taken place from the cold war and tension to détente, to the normalization of relations between countries with differing social systems. The consistent fulfillment of the Peace Program has helped to settle key world problems, consolidate the foundations of world peace and security, make the trend toward détente the overriding feature of the international situation, and reduce the threat of another world war.

Based on a dependable scientific foundation, on an account of key sociopolitical factors, the alignment of class forces in the world, and other cardinal foreign political conditions, the policy pursued by the Soviet Union on the international scene together with the other countries of the socialist community has led to results of truly historic significance: to the creation of favorable new possibilities facilitating the successful work of the peoples for peace, democracy, and social progress.

The CPSU Central Committee's Report gave a vivid panorama of the changes that have taken place in the world situation during the past five years and put forward new general foreign policy aims.

Long-standing objectives were achieved during that period, thanks to socialism's strengthened position, unity, and mutual support among the socialist countries. A glorious victory has been won by the people of Vietnam, who attained independence and national unity. Laos and Democratic Kampuchea have achieved freedom. Worldwide recognition of the German Democratic Republic's sovereignty, the international reaffirmation of the inviolability of the western frontiers of the GDR, Poland, and Czechoslovakia, and the legal fixing of the main results of the liberation struggle of the European peoples during and after the Second World War are some of the tangible results of the concerted efforts of the socialist countries that have created the conditions for durable peace and good-neighborly cooperation in and outside Europe. Socialism has been firmly established in Cuba, whose international position and prestige have been enhanced.

The developments of the past five years have shown that on an international plane socialism brings peace, respect for the sovereignty of all nations, and equal interstate relations, that it is the mainstay of the peoples fighting for freedom and independence. The socialist countries' beneficial influence on the course of world developments is becoming ever broader and deeper. The Central Committee's report gave a picture of close political, economic, and ideological cooperation among the socialist countries, cooperation that is the primary condition of their common success in the struggle for world peace and security.

The efficient alliance of the communist parties of the socialist countries, community of their world outlook, aims, and will are the foundation and motive force of this cooperation. The leaders of these communist parties maintain constant contacts and systematically consult each other on major problems and jointly chart the programs for their further progress.

The Warsaw Treaty Political Consultative Committee is one of the principal instruments of cooperation among the socialist countries. Many of its initiatives have underlain the decisions adopted by international forums or found reflection in a number of bilateral international acts. The Warsaw Treaty organization serves peace and socialism, and as long as the NATO bloc exists the Soviet Union and the other members of the Warsaw Treaty are determined to strengthen their military and political alliance.

Economic cooperation among the member states of the socialist community enhances its material foundation. The implementation of the comprehensive program of socialist economic integration is raising this cooperation to a higher level, promoting the interaction of the member states' economies and making them mutually complementary and beneficial. The Soviet Union's trade with the other CMEA countries is expanding rapidly, more than doubling during the past five years. Of great importance for the solution of key problems such as satisfying the growing requirements in energy, fuel, and basic raw materials, raising the level of the engineering industry, and more fully meeting the demands for food and consumer goods will be special purpose long-term programs.

The ideological cooperation between the fraternal parties is expanding, thereby helping to raise the level of ideological and educational work in each party and wage the struggle against capitalist ideology with growing success. Today many areas of science are developing through the collective efforts by the scientists of the socialist countries; cooperation in the field of mass media is also increasing.

The enhanced unity of the socialist countries on the basis of Marxist-Leninist principles of socialist internationalism, equality, and comradely cooperation facilitates the strengthening of their international position and the solution of major problems of today. "In its relations with the socialist countries," Leonid Brezhnev said at the Twenty-fifth Congress, "the CPSU firmly follows the tested rule of working in the spirit of true equality and interest in each other's successes, of working out decisions that meet international, as well as national, interests."

This stand is highly appreciated in the fraternal countries, which attach primary significance to the further development and strengthening of the socialist community and to the all-sided cooperation with the Soviet Union.

In its efforts to safeguard world peace and security the Soviet Union pays much attention to strengthening and comprehensively promoting relations with the developing countries. The decisions of the Twenty-fifth Congress reaffirm the CPSU's principled policy of furthering these relations, backing peoples defending their freedom, and of consolidating solidarity with the forces of progress, democracy, and national independence in the developing countries. At the Twenty-fifth Congress Leonid Brezhnev noted:

> We are brought together with the vast majority of the states, that arose on the ruins of the colonial system, by our deep common allegiance to peace and freedom, and aversion to all forms of aggression and domination, and to exploitation of one country by another. This community of basic aspirations is rich and fruitful soil on which our friendship will continue to grow and flourish!

The developing countries are playing a growing role in world events, gaining increasing influence, and activating their foreign policies. The present alignment of world forces enables these countries to resist imperialist dictation more successfully and secure just and equal economic relations. They are making a large contribution to the common struggle for world peace and security, and this contribution can be even greater.

In pressing for the consolidation of the principles of peaceful coexistence with capitalist countries, Soviet diplomacy has made noticeable progress during the past five years towards a turn from the cold war to détente, from the threat of war to peaceful cooperation. These five years have witnessed an improvement of the USSR's relations with the West

European states. Cooperation has been successfully developing with France, a considerable positive change has taken place in relations with the FRG, and relations with Britain, Italy, and other West European countries have also acquired a positive character. As was pointed out at the Twenty-fifth CPSU Congress, virtually not a single state in Western Europe has held aloof from the broad process of normalizing relations with socialist countries.

Important multilateral measures have been taken. The success of the European Conference made it possible to create favorable conditions for maintaining and strengthening peace in Europe and to map out prospects for peaceful cooperation in many fields. The collective reaffirmation of the inviolability of the existing frontiers in Europe and the elaboration and formalization of a code of principles of interstate relations in the Final Act were a major achievement in the efforts to establish peaceful relations in Europe.

In parallel with Soviet foreign policy activity in Europe, our diplomacy has been active in other areas. Soviet-Canadian relations have become more versatile, relations with Latin American states have been extended, and relations with Japan, with whom the Soviet Union wants good-neighborly and friendly relations, are on the whole improving.

In the complex of the Soviet Union's relations with capitalist countries the most important place justly belongs to relations with the United States, the largest power of the capitalist world. The improvement of these relations was the decisive factor in strengthening peace and reducing the threat of another war. Soviet and U.S. leaders have reached an understanding on the need for peaceful and equal relations. Documents such as the Basic Principles of Mutual Relations Between the USSR and the USA, the Agreement on the Prevention of Nuclear War,* and the treaties and agreements restricting strategic armaments have laid a solid political and legal foundation for the promotion of mutually beneficial cooperation between the two countries on the principles of peaceful coexistence, and have to some extent reduced the threat of a nuclear war. Soviet-American relations are developing in many spheres: the two countries are exchanging

---

* The agreement was signed in 1973.

various delegations, expanding cultural exchanges, and giving effect to their agreements on economic, scientific, and technical cooperation.*

The positive results of the Soviet Union's constructive policy of peace and the consistent implementation of the Leninist foreign policy principles and the Peace Program are thus to be seen in a wide spectrum of its international relations. Needless to say, the content and character of international relations do not depend solely on the Soviet Union and the other socialist countries. Various forces are active on the international scene and one cannot fail to see the negative influence of certain circles in the capitalist countries on the situation in the world. The intrigues of these forces were appropriately analyzed in the Report of the Central Committee.

Some influential circles in the West European countries are reluctant to abandon the cold war mentality and to pursue consistently a policy of mutually beneficial cooperation and noninterference in the affairs of other countries. For instance, in the Federal Republic of Germany revenge-seeking right wing forces are attacking the policy of normalizing relations with the socialist countries. In Japan, some circles are endeavoring to make groundless and unlawful claims on the Soviet Union. In the U.S., the influential forces opposed to détente are seeking to obstruct the development of Soviet-U.S. relations, step up the arms race in the U.S. and in NATO, and interfere in the internal affairs of the USSR and other socialist countries.

The adversaries of an improved international climate in Europe are trying to emasculate and distort the Final Act of the European Conference and use it for anticommunist and anti-Soviet demagoguery. Many newspapers, radio and TV stations in the West are fanning hostility toward socialist countries and hindering the strengthening of mutual trust and the development of cooperation. . . .

Despite the overall improvement of the international climate, the intrigues of the enemies of world peace and security remain a source of military threats and of the precipitation and exacerbation of conflicts and crises. Ag-

---

* It has to be pointed out that the above-mentioned facts date back to the period of détente.

gressive imperialist circles are spurring the arms race and spreading the myth about the "Soviet threat"; they are swelling military budgets and filling their arsenals with new deadly weapons. Although the change in the alignment of world forces has considerably reduced their possibilities for unleashing acts of aggression, the nature of imperialism has remained immutable. For this reason there is a constant need for unremitting vigilance, active efforts in defense of peace, a further improvement of the international situation and the total expulsion of the cold war spirit from international life.

The Twenty-fifth Congress of the CPSU charted a broad program for the further struggle for peace and international cooperation, for the freedom and independence of nations. This program organically stems from, and is an elaboration of, the Peace Program adopted by the Twenty-fourth Congress. The tasks outlined in the report delivered by the general secretary of the CPSU Central Committee, Leonid Brezhnev, were dictated by the course of world events, by the present stage of the development of international relations. They rest on the results that have been achieved, on the radical changes that have taken place on the international scene in recent years, and are aimed at attaining further progress in the drive to assure a peaceful future for mankind and to eliminate wars from the life of human society.

This Program envisages, above all, an increased joint contribution by the fraternal socialist states to the consolidation of peace and the expansion of all-sided cooperation among them in the building of a new society. The Soviet Union will continue to work for an end to the arms race and for a transition to a cutback in the stockpiles of weapons—to disarmament. A series of concrete steps have been planned to accomplish this cardinal task. The Soviet Union will do everything in its power to complete the preparations for a new agreement with the U.S. on limiting and reducing strategic armaments and for the conclusion of international treaties on a general and complete cessation of nuclear tests; on banning and destroying chemical weapons; and on banning the development of new types and systems of weapons of mass annihilation and of actions influencing the environment for military and other hostile purposes. It is planned to take new steps to invigorate the talks on a cutback of armed forces and arms in Central Europe and instead of the growth of the military expenditures of many countries, secure a systematic reduction of these expenditures, and convene a World Disarmament Conference as soon as possible.

The Program calls for concentrated efforts of the peace-loving states to eradicate the remaining flashpoints of war, including the one in the Middle East. In the Report to the Congress Leonid Brezhnev said that the USSR was prepared to join in the quest for a solution of such a problem as the ending of the arms race in that region.

Moreover, the Program calls for a deepening of the détente, for giving it the concrete form of mutually beneficial cooperation between states, and for the full implementation of the Final Act of the European Conference. In keeping with the principles of peaceful coexistence, the USSR will consistently expand long-term, mutually advantageous political, economic, scientific, and cultural cooperation with the U.S., France, the FRG, Great Britain, Italy, Canada, Japan, and other capitalist countries.

The documents adopted by the Congress underscore that security in Asia must be ensured through the joint efforts of the countries of that continent. The Soviet Union has set its sights on the conclusion of a worldwide treaty on the nonuse of force in international relations, under which the signatories, including the nuclear powers, will pledge to refrain from using any types of weapons, including nuclear weapons, for the settlement of disputes between them.

One of the central international tasks put forward at the twenty-fifth Congress is the total abolition of all remnants of the system of colonial oppression, the infringement on the equality and independence of nations, and the eradication of hotbeds of colonialism and racism.

Lastly, the Congress declared that the Soviet Union was determined to work for the removal of discrimination and all artificial barriers in international trade, and the abolition of all manifestations of inequality, dictation, and exploitation in international economic relations.

The Program for the further struggle for peace and international cooperation and for the freedom and independence of nations put forward by the twenty-fifth Congress mirrors not only the Soviet Union's ardent desire for peace, not only its consistent policy of peace, but also the realism and unequivocal concreteness of its foreign policy, which pursues practical aims that meet the vital requirements of our times. In bourgeois countries, there are many politicians and statesmen who are quite willing to speak about peace and proclaim the finest intentions in this respect. But in practice one finds out that what they say are merely empty phrases, that their words are not backed by practical steps leading to peace. The words of the CPSU are not at variance with its deeds. In the period between the twenty-fourth and twenty-fifth Congresses the world was given further eloquent proof that the Peace Program adopted by the CPSU became the platform of active and purposeful actions, that it was steadfastly translated into life, and embodied in concrete results, in tangible changes for the better on the world scene. The CPSU undeviatingly abides by Lenin's behest to initiate as many decisions and steps as possible that would lead to peace, if not to the complete elimination of the war danger.

There is no doubt whatsoever that the new foreign policy program formulated by the twenty-fifth Congress will provide the impetus for further positive changes in the international situation and exercise a beneficial influence on world developments.

To the Congress of the Communist Party of Denmark

Traditionally, Communists of different countries invite delegations of Communist and Worker's Parties to their Party Congresses. The guests use these opportunities to inform their listeners about the latest events in their country, about their party's progress, achievements in the economy, and their relationship with other parties. The following is an excerpt from the speech delivered by the head of the Soviet delegation, Konstantin U. Chernenko, at the Twenty-fifth Congress of the Communist Party of Denmark on September 24, 1976.

The creative, constructive character of the activity carried out by our Party and people at home determines the peace-loving character of the Soviet state's policy in the international arena.

You know, of course, that the twenty-fifth Congress of the Communist Party of the Soviet Union endorsed the Program of further struggle for peace and international co-operation, and for the freedom and independence of the peoples. Our Party and its Central Committee do everything they can to ensure that this program is consistently implemented. We have been steadily working toward this goal, coordinating our efforts, as always, with the efforts of fraternal socialist countries, strengthening solidarity with Communist and Workers' parties and cooperating with all forces who stand for peace and progress.

We regard it as a most important task today to promote the positive trends in the international arena and impart to the process of détente an irreversible character. This is a

32

complicated and many-sided task. It is necessary above all to achieve positive results in curbing the arms race and to complement political détente with military détente.

The Soviet Union, like the other countries of the socialist community, is actively and consistently pursuing a course of carrying out in full the Final Act of the Conference on Security and Cooperation in Europe adopted in Helsinki. We proceed here from the belief that implementation of the accords reached there is in the interests of all nations.

That is why we resolutely reject the attempts of certain forces in the West to hinder efforts aimed at solving the questions raised in Helsinki and arbitrarily to interpret and distort the essence of the Final Act, to oppose some of its principles to others. Regrettably, vacillations and inconsistency in this matter can sometimes be observed even in those leaders who themselves contributed to détente at its first stages.

Such inconsistency, in the final analysis, plays into the hands of the aggressive forces, those who would like to drag the world back to the times of the cold war.

Lasting Peace and Reliable Security for Europe

This article, which was first published in the journal International Affairs *(no. 4, April 1978), is dedicated to the results of the Belgrade Meeting of the representatives of countries participating in the Helsinki Conference. In the course of the Belgrade Meeting, held in accordance with the stipulations of the Helsinki Final Act, representatives of the 33 European countries, the United States, and Canada exchanged opinions on the problems of strengthening security, developing cooperation in Europe, and further consolidating détente.*

A meeting of the representatives of the countries that participated in the Conference on Security and Cooperation in Europe completed its work in Belgrade in early March. It convened in October 1977 in accordance with the provisions of the Helsinki Final Act on follow-up measures. In the course of the Belgrade meeting the representatives of 33 European states, the U.S., and Canada had a broad exchange of views on the implementation of the provisions of the Final Act, the improvement of relations between countries, the consolidation of security and the development of cooperation on the continent, and the future of détente. The delegations set out the views of their governments on these issues. Many of them, above all, the delegations from the Soviet Union and the other socialist countries, made proposals aimed at further easing international tensions and reiterated their determination to advance along the road mapped out in Helsinki.

The Belgrade meeting stressed the historic importance and political significance of the Helsinki Conference, and provided a new impetus toward implementing the provisions of the Final Act. The USSR and the other countries of the socialist community, acting in accordance with their principled line of strengthening détente, put forward for discussion a constructive program for consolidating security and developing cooperation in Europe, and made active efforts to ensure that a truly meaningful final document was worked out by the meeting.

It should also be pointed out that the Belgrade meeting reflected certain experience in the implementation of the Final Act, as well as difficulties stemming from the desire of certain circles in the West to revise the provisions of that document and use it as an instrument for interfering in the affairs of other states. It has to be stated that not all the participants in the Belgrade meeting always displayed a constructive approach to its work. For instance, the delegations from the United States and its partners in the NATO military bloc tried to divert this forum from discussion of the main problems, distort the letter and spirit of the Final Act, and include in the final document of the Belgrade meeting provisions to legalize interference in the internal affairs of the socialist states, on the pretext of "defending human rights." These attempts, however, met with utter failure and the meeting could not be sidetracked from the main issues connected with the further development of détente and consolidation of security in Europe. The attempts by the representatives of the U.S. and some Western powers to have the meeting sow the seeds of dissension and suspicion, instead of strengthening cooperation, also completely failed.

A final document was adopted at the Belgrade meeting. Its provisions are aimed at continuing the process of détente and expansion of cooperation, begun by the heads of state and government in Helsinki in 1975. The document underlines the importance the representatives of the participant states attach to détente, which has continued since the conclusion of the Final Act, in spite of difficulties and obstacles. In this context they stressed the role of the Conference on Security and Cooperation in Europe, meaning that the implementation of the provisions of the Final Act is of vital importance for the development of this process. The final document confirms the resolution of the governments of the participant countries completely to fulfill all the provisions of the Final Act on a unilateral, a bilateral, and a multilateral basis. It envisages meetings of experts to examine and develop a generally acceptable method for the peaceful settlement of disputes among states, to prepare a European scientific forum, and to look into ways and means to contribute to the concrete initiatives for mutually beneficial economic, scientific, and cultural cooperation in the Mediterranean. The next Belgrade-type meeting is to be held in Madrid in November 1980.*

Less than three years have passed since the conclusion of the Helsinki Conference on Security and Cooperation in Europe. This period has brought vivid proof of the historic significance of that event for the nations of our continent. The Conference opened up a new stage in the easing of international tensions, adoption of the principles of peaceful coexistence between states with different social systems, and development of contacts and ties between them in the political, economic, scientific, technical, cultural, and other fields.

In keeping with its Leninist policy of peaceful coexistence, the Soviet Union has consistently pursued an international line for implementing all the principles and accords of the Final Act in their totality. This has fully conformed to the foreign policy Program of Further Struggle for Peace and International Cooperation, and for the Freedom and Independence of the Peoples adopted by the Twenty-fifth Congress of the CPSU. One of the tasks set in the Program is to "do everything to deepen international détente, to embody it in concrete forms of mutually beneficial cooperation between states. Work vigorously for the full implementation of the Final Act of the European Conference, and for greater peaceful cooperation in Europe."

The coordination of the foreign policy moves by the Soviet Union and the other socialist countries has far-reaching significance for the implementation of the Helsinki accords and for the general strengthening of world peace and security. The socialist countries have many times put forward joint proposals aimed at strengthening détente and developing the positive achievements made in Helsinki.

In the course of their bilateral and multilateral meetings after Helsinki, the leaders of the fraternal socialist countries

---

* The Madrid Conference of the States participating in the Conference on Security and Cooperation in Europe was held from November 11, 1980 to September 9, 1983.

have repeatedly reaffirmed their determination to abide by and implement all the provisions of the Final Act. At the meeting of their Political Consultative Committee in November 1976, the Warsaw Treaty states pledged their continued adherence to a concerted course for peace and security in Europe and the world, for consolidating détente, and promoting the principles of peaceful coexistence. They appealed to all the participants in the Helsinki Conference to implement the provisions of the Final Act actively and fully.

The meeting of the Warsaw Treaty Committee of Foreign Ministers in May 1977 reiterated the readiness of the socialist countries for the all-round cooperation with all the signatory countries of the Helsinki accords in fulfilling the tasks set by them. The meeting also proclaimed their resolve to ensure constructive work at the Belgrade meeting in order to expand, deepen, and make continuous and lasting the process of détente.

The progressive and democratic forces in the European countries play an important role in the development of détente by calling on their governments strictly to observe the Helsinki principles and accords. The Berlin Forum of the European Communists in June 1976 stated that "to guarantee the durability of détente and to strengthen and extend it further, the decisions adopted in Helsinki must be supported and sustained by the struggle of the masses of the people to implement them fully and completely, to curb and push back the reactionary forces, who reject the results of the Conference on Security and Cooperation in Europe and who seek to thwart the course towards détente and security for the peoples."

A considerable success of the policy of détente is the achievement of an agreed and mutually acceptable approach by the USSR and the other socialist countries and by a number of Western countries to the implementation of the Final Act as a result of talks between their leaders. This approach consists in the need to honor the principles of relations between states as proclaimed by the European Conference and to implement all the provisions of the Final Act. Such an approach was proclaimed, in particular, in the Soviet-French declaration of 1975. It is also reflected in the Soviet agreements with Italy, Portugal, Britain, Turkey, Finland, Belgium, Denmark, and some other Western participants in the Helsinki Conference.

A major event was the signing of the joint Soviet-French statement on détente as a result of Leonid Brezhnev's visit to France in the summer of 1977. In that first bilateral document dealing specifically with the problem of détenete, the USSR and France clearly stated the vital need for the policy of détente and their determination to continue to work actively to promote it.

The Soviet Union and the fraternal socialist states, acting in strict compliance with the letter and spirt of the Helsinki accords, have worked vigorously and persistently to make détente tangible and spread it to other regions of the world.

Following the Helsinki Conference, the Soviet Union and the other socialist countries put forward a series of initiatives aimed at expanding and deepening détente, limiting the arms race, reducing the threat of war, and promoting cooperation in Europe. One fundamental aim of these activities has been to make the basic principles of relations between states that form the political foundation of the Final Act more effective and immutable international law. After Helsinki political contacts and consultations between the states belonging to the two social systems have markedly expanded and diversified. Of signal importance in this connection are the summit talks and Leonid Brezhnev's meetings with the Western heads of state and government, which contribute to greater mutual trust and political cooperation in various fields.

The Soviet Union has made an immense contribution to improving present-day international relations by affirming the Leninist principles of peaceful coexistence, the main goals and principles of its foreign policy, in its new Constitution. For the first time ever, the Fundamental Law of a state has incorporated the principles of relations between states contained in the Helsinki Final Act. The first socialist country in the world has thereby convincingly demonstrated its sincere striving toward peaceful coexistence between states with different social systems as an immutable law of international life.

In the period between Helsinki and Belgrade, the states that participated in the European Conference have done much for expanding bilateral cooperation in various fields. In this period, for example, the USSR signed agreements, including long-term ones, in various fields of economic, scientific, and technical cooperation with France, Italy, Belgium, Portugal,

Canada, Finland, Cyprus, Turkey, and other countries. The volume of Soviet foreign trade has increased by some 40 percent since 1974.

Considerable achievements have been made in cultural and humanitarian links. Agreements have been concluded on cultural cooperation between the USSR, on the one hand, and the U.S., Japan, the Federal Republic of Germany, Belgium, and other countries, on the other. In accordance with the provisions of the Final Act, the USSR has facilitated entry and exit formalities for citizens on private or business trips. Additional measures have been taken to improve the conditions in which foreign journalists work.

The Soviet mass media have tirelessly propagated the ideas of peace, friendship, and mutual understanding among peoples in strict accordance with the concept of cooperation among states in culture and education, the spread of information, and human contacts in the context of deepening détente, the concept that was agreed upon at the Helsinki Conference.

By developing their business links with the Western partners, the Soviet Union and the other socialist countries have sought actively to implement the provisions of the Final Act on multilateral cooperation. This goal is furthered, among other things, by the Soviet proposals to hold European congresses or interstate conferences on energy, transport, and environmental protection, as well as by the initiatives of the socialist countries aimed at establishing relations between the Council for Mutual Economic Assistance [CMEA] and the European Economic Community [EEC].

The Soviet Union and the other socialist countries have exerted considerable efforts to bring about a halt in the arms race, take measures to limit arms and promote disarmament, and to back up political détente with military détente, all in the spirit of Helsinki. This is the aim, for example, of the November 1976 proposal by the Warsaw Treaty states to all the participants in the European Conference to conclude a treaty on not being the first to use nuclear weapons against one another and not increasing the membership of the Warsaw Treaty and NATO.

Another major initiative aimed at accomplishing the tasks set by the Helsinki Conference is the Soviet platform of action proposed in October 1977 to consolidate military détente in

Europe, which provided for a series of joint measures by the states that participated in the Conference.

In keeping with the Helsinki decisions on measures to build confidence among nations, the socialist countries have given prior notification of major military exercises and have invited foreign military observers. For example, military representatives from the U.S., Great Britain, Benelux,* and other countries have been invited to the maneuvers by Soviet troops code-named Berezina in the area of Minsk, Orsha, and Polotsk in 1978.

The Soviet Union has come out with a number of important proposals aimed at curbing the arms race, consolidating peace, and achieving the historic task of the Helsinki Conference—to make détente an irreversible process and spread it to other regions of the world. They include proposals for a world treaty on the nonuse of force in international relations; for all states simultaneously to put an end to the production of nuclear weapons and subsequently reduce and completely eliminate them; for mutual renunciation of the production of the neutron weapons; for banning nuclear weapons tests along with a moratorium on peaceful nuclear explosions. Our country regards the successful conclusion of the ongoing talks and the signing of a Soviet-U.S. treaty on limiting strategic arms and a treaty on reduction of arms and troops cuts in Central Europe as being of high priority. The Soviet Union is demonstrating its readiness to reduce and eliminate the threat of nuclear war, to curb the arms race, and to strengthen security on the European continent and throughout the world.

Thus, after Helsinki the Soviet Union and the other socialist countries have carried out a vast amount of work to implement the decisions of the European Conference. It should be borne in mind, however, that the Final Act is a long-term program for turning Europe into a continent of lasting peace, security, and cooperation, and progress in this direction will greatly depend on the advance of the cause of détente. . . .

The time that has passed since the European Conference has shown that the Soviet Union has been acting purposefully and persistently to consolidate and extend détente, in accordance with its principled line to bring about peaceful coexistence

---

* Belgium, the Netherlands, Luxembourg.

between states with different social systems and promote all-round cooperation to ensure a peaceful future for nations. . . .

For all the unquestionable success of the policy of peaceful coexistence, the fact remains that, since the Helsinki Conference, the aggressive and reactionary forces of imperialism have noticeably intensified their intrigues. They seek to revive an atmosphere of mistrust between states, maintain and whip up tensions, and speed up the arms race, and are assiduously spreading the lie about a "Soviet military threat." They have unleashed a slanderous campaign over an imagined "human rights" problem in the socialist countries in an effort to distort the provisions of the Final Act and literally legalize their attempts at interference in the socialist countries' internal affairs.

The imperialist line of opposing and disrupting détente is clearly manifested in the arms race, which is being whipped up by NATO. To justify this, imperialist reactionaries are trying to misrepresent the peaceful initiatives of the Soviet Union and the other socialist countries and to distort the meaning of their purely defensive measures. There has never been any "Soviet military threat."

In a bid to undermine the policy of détente, the reactionary forces have, in the post-Helsinki period, tried to misinterpret the Final Act and make its realization lopsided, claiming the role of "monitors" of the Helsinki accords, in other (but not their own) countries, which contradicts the results of the Conference achieved through the joint efforts of 35 states.

The Belgrade Meeting* naturally reflected the clash between the main trends in present-day international affairs. One is that of consolidating and deepening détente and realizing the full range of provisions and accords included in the Final Act, in the name of peace and security in Europe and broader all-round cooperation between the states of the continent. The other trend is undermining détente, seeking to revise the Final Act and interpret it in a one-sided way in order to interfere in the internal affairs of other states.

The Soviet Union regarded the Belgrade Meeting as a working forum for a positive multilateral exchange of views on how to further détente and cooperation among states. . . .

---

* A meeting of representatives of the 35 states participating in the Helsinki Conference was held from October 4, 1977 to March 9, 1978 in Belgrade. This was the first major step toward implementing the Final Act signed in Helsinki.

The Soviet Union and the other socialist countries came to the Belgrade Meeting with a constructive program aimed at further strengthening peace and security in Europe and developing cooperation among states, a program based on experience in implementing the Helsinki decisions. During the meeting, the Soviet delegation repeatedly stated that the main direction of the many-sided process initiated in Helsinki has always been to strengthen security and expand cooperation in Europe, avert a thermonuclear war, halt the arms race, and take disarmament measures. It was in the light of these tasks that the Soviet delegation in Belgrade assessed the proposals made by other delegations and approached the drafting of the Meeting's final document.

The Soviet Union submitted to the Belgrade Meeting a platform of action to consolidate military détente in Europe. It called upon the participants in the Helsinki Conference to sign a treaty on not being the first to use nuclear weapons against one another, to agree not to expand the opposing military and political groupings and alliances in Europe by admitting new members, to continue to implement the measures outlined in the Final Act, such as giving notification of major military exercises, inviting observers to some exercises, and exchanging military delegations. The USSR proposed that military exercises should not involve more than a certain number of troops (50–60,000). It has also declared its support for spreading the military confidence-building measure taken in Helsinki to the southern Mediterranean countries subject, of course, to the consent of these countries. This platform of action is an important contribution to tackling the problem of complementing political détente with military détente.

The USSR and Poland put forward a joint proposal to consolidate the Final Act's ten principles through legislation. Other socialist countries also launched important initiatives at the Belgrade Meeting. The Bulgarian delegation made a proposal to support the 1978 Special UN General Assembly Session on Disarmament and to speed up the preparations for a World Disarmament Conference; the GDR delegation proposed that the participating states renounce the production of neutron nuclear warheads and the Rumanian delegation proposed a freeze on their military budgets at the 1977 or 1978 level.

Some other states, including neutral countries, also made constructive proposals at the Belgrade Meeting. A proposal for strengthening European security and disarmament made by nine neutral and nonaligned countries was met with interest. The document emphasized the importance and urgency of effective measures to end the arms race and invigorate the talks at various forums dealing with arms limitation and disarmament, and recognized the need to take urgent steps towards these goals on a regional basis, especially in Europe where major military potentials are concentrated.

All these proposals shared a common concern for the security of the peoples of Europe and for ensuring Europeans the basic human right—that to a peaceful life.

By all their activities at the Belgrade Meeting, the Soviet Union and the other socialist states showed that they resolutely oppose attempts to revise the provisions of the Final Act and will continue to strive for implementation by all countries the agreements achieved in Helsinki.

The representatives of the U.S. and its NATO allies, however, opposed these proposals whose implementation not only would not damage the security of any country but would strengthen the security of everyone, help to avert the danger of a nuclear conflict and reduce burdensome military spending. The Western delegates used various pretexts to avoid serious discussion of the topical questions of limiting the arms race and disarmament and of taking effective measures to improve European security. The U.S. delegate, Arthur Goldberg, said bluntly that the disarmament proposals of the socialist countries should not be discussed at the Belgrade meeting. Others tried to sidetrack the debate by turning to secondary matters, emphasizing, for example, the regulations on participation of observers in military exercises.

The U.S. delegation in Belgrade reacted with irritation to speeches condemning plans to manufacture neutron weapons in the U.S. and deploy them in Western Europe. It ignored the fact that, in proposing to renounce the manufacture of the neutron weapons, the Soviet Union itself is ready to undertake firm commitments in this respect. Attempts are being made, however, to conceal this fact from the public in Western countries. But this proposal, like the platform of action to consolidate military détente in Europe put forward by the

USSR, provides for mutual pledges by states that would cause no damage to any of them and would contribute to universal security.

In view of the vital importance of all these problems, the delegations of the USSR and the other socialist countries proposed including in the final document of the Belgrade Meeting a provision on the advisability of considering all questions of military détente, including confidence measures, within the framework of bodies of specialists and experts set up for the express purpose of preparing corresponding decisions for governments. The delegations of the U.S. and its NATO allies, however, refused to include this in the final document.

Nevertheless, in discussing questions of European security, many participants in the Belgrade meeting underlined the importance and urgency for all states of concrete measures to end the arms race and continue the efforts at various arms limitation and disarmament forums with a view to general and complete disarmament under strict and effective international control. In this connection, full support for the Special UN General Assembly Session on Disarmament planned for the spring of 1978 was particularly stressed.

High on the agenda of the Belgrade Meeting was the subject of cooperation in the economy, science, and technology and environmental protection. Taking note of the favorable development of trade and economic cooperation between them, the participating states admitted, however, that it did not yet correspond to the full potential. They spoke in favor of fresh efforts to ensure the full implementation of the provisions of the Final Act, notably in the field of business contacts and economic information. The desire was expressed to develop trade more rapidly through a diversification of its structure, to continue efforts, on a mutual basis, to reduce or gradually eliminate all sorts of trade barriers and to avoid, as far as possible, the creation of new obstacles.

Many countries at the Belgrade Meeting voiced their concern over the pollution of the environment in some regions. At the same time satisfaction was expressed with cooperation in the field of environmental protection, particularly within the framework of the UN. The participants in the meeting reaffirmed their intention to continue cooperation in protecting and improving the environment.

The USSR delegation in Belgrade made a proposal on the development of European cooperation in energy, transport, and environmental protection. In this connection, the practical importance of European congresses or interstate conferences on these problems for Europe was stressed. An important role in this could be played by the Economic Commission for Europe, as well as UNESCO, which deals with cooperation in education, science, and culture.

The position of the socialist countries and a number of Western countries on the development of humanitarian links between the participants of the European Conference in the spirit of the Helsinki accords was marked by a businesslike and constructive approach. Impressive figures were cited in Belgrade on the growing exchange of cultural values, scientific contacts, and tourism. These were not, however, the questions that interested some Western delegations in the discussion of humanitarian issues. They preferred to use this section of the Final Act to launch propaganda attacks against the Soviet Union and the other socialist countries.

Although the main task of the Belgrade Meeting, as recorded in its agenda, was to discuss ways of improving relations between countries, promoting security and cooperation in Europe, and developing détente in the future, the delegations of the U.S. and some of its NATO allies tried to bypass these questions and divert the Meeting from the tasks formulated in Helsinki toward interference in the internal affairs of states, in violation of the letter and spirit of the Helsinki accords. The head of the U.S. delegation went out of his way to force a "human rights" debate on the meeting to justify the pretext for interference in the internal affairs of the socialist countries. He insisted that the final document of the Meeting should deal with the so-called "third basket" in virtual disregard of important issues of détente. The Soviet Union, however, and other participants in the Meeting rejected attempts to distort the provisions of the Final Act and to replace them with irrelevant provisions, and to use the Helsinki accords for selfish ends. In Belgrade all attempts to revise the Final Act and distort its meaning were frustrated.

The overwhelming majority of the delegates rightly believe that the Helsinki decisions were the sole compass for the Belgrade Meeting. The Final Act cannot be in any way replaced. It would be a dangerous delusion to believe that the

Belgrade Meeting, which was a working forum of the representatives of foreign ministers, should seek an alternative to the fundamental program agreed upon by the leaders of 35 countries in Helsinki. The Soviet Union is convinced that the historic document adopted at Helsinki reflects an agreed and generally recognized basis for further development of relations between states and their efforts to consolidate peace and security in Europe. The principles proclaimed in Helsinki are of permanent value and will determine the future development of relations between states.

Despite maneuvers by certain circles which tried to reduce the importance of the Helsinki accords, the Belgrade Meeting has come to a constructive conclusion. All attempts to push it off the main road to détente have failed. It has demonstrated that the principles and provisions of the Final Act have taken deep root in international relations and have gained wide recognition, so they cannot be rejected or canceled. The Belgrade Meeting summed up the results of development of international relations in the post-Helsinki period. It became clear at the Meeting how much work the Soviet Union and other countries have done to implement the provisions of the Final Act in the fields of economic relations, scientific, and cultural ties, and measures aimed at reducing international tensions and normalizing relations between nations. It is therefore no accident that the countries genuinely acting in the spirit of Helsinki are those consistently implementing Leninist foreign policy principles. The meeting in Belgrade showed the way to further advance in the cause of strengthening European security. The resolution of states to develop cooperation opens up new horizons for implementing the agreements achieved in Helsinki.

On this basis there is every ground to believe that the Meeting is of major positive significance as a stage in the implementation of the Helsinki program. It will undoubtedly have a positive effect on the process of consolidating security and developing cooperation in Europe.

The Soviet Union and the fraternal socialist countries are concentrating their efforts on averting the danger of a nuclear war; making the positive international changes stable; expanding and consolidating détente, making its development irreversible; and halting the arms race. Of immense significance in this respect is the implementation of the Final Act by all the participants in the Helsinki Conference in all its sections. This was the Soviet Union's persistent stand at the Belgrade Meeting.

We in this country view the consistent implementation of the decisions of the European Conference as the way to shape a new face of Europe, to make it a continent of lasting peace, security, and fruitful cooperation.

The time since the Helsinki Conference has shown that military confidence-building measures alone cannot bring about dramatic improvement in the situation in Europe and the world unless there is progress toward limiting arms and towards disarmament. The level of European security already achieved is not the limit, but rather the beginning. We would like to defuse the nuclear and gunpowder storehouse that Europe now is. This is, of course, no simple task, but a start should be made at least to prevent the emergence there of new types of mass destruction weapons, including the neutron weapons, and then go on to bring down the level of military confrontation. Such measures of military détente would do much to consolidate political détente. The socialist countries oppose on principle the division of the world into military blocs and have more than once voiced their readiness simultaneously to disband the Warsaw Treaty and the North Atlantic Treaty Organization or, as a preliminary step, to abolish their military organizations.

It is also of exceptional importance to create the material framework of peaceful cooperation in Europe through the expansion of ties and establishment of contacts between European nations and states in the economy, science, and technology, and cultural and humanitarian fields.

The vigorous peace policy pursued by the Soviet Union, the fraternal socialist countries, and the drive for peace by all the progressive forces have made détente a reality of our time. It is the logical result of the development of relations between states with different social systems on the basis of peaceful coexistence and can be essentially consolidated through the expansion of trade, business, scientific, and cultural contacts between countries. It is, however, impossible not to see that détente is a complex process. Its course depends not only on the condition of interstate relations but also on economic, social, and ideological factors. This does not mean, however, that this process is fading out. Far from it, it gains increasing support from peoples who pin their hopes of lasting peace on détente.

The main achievement of the Belgrade Meeting is that it has demonstrated the resoluteness of the European nations to continue to pursue the line worked out in Helsinki, where a new stage was begun in détente, consolidating the principles of peaceful coexistence and cooperation between states of the two opposing social systems.

The Soviet Union, together with the fraternal socialist countries, is ready to do everything possible to help developments on our continent to lead to the elimination of the military threat, and to the creation of an atmosphere of confidence in the inevitability of its peaceful future, as well as to an expansion of all-round cooperation between states for the good of the peoples.

To the Congress of the Communist Party of Greece

The following is an excerpt from the speech delivered on May 16, 1978, when Konstantin U. Chernenko headed the Soviet Communist Party delegation at the Tenth Congress of the Communist Party of Greece. In his speech he focused on the problems of Europe. In particular he spoke for solving by peaceful means all the disputable problems among the countries of the Mediterranean.

Comrades, the essence of the Leninist foreign policy of the Soviet state is well known to you. Our policy line, to put it briefly, has been and remains one of struggle for peace among nations, for the stable and lasting security of all countries on our planet. To solve this problem we are working together with the peoples of the fraternal socialist countries. The working-class movement and above all the communist parties are a major force fighting for peace. We highly appreciate the contribution made by the communists of our continent to the cause of strengthening peace, and in this context we attach great importance to the results of the Berlin Conference of 1976. A significant role in world development today is played by the cooperation between countries of socialism and countries liberated from colonial oppression. We also take into account the role played by realistically minded circles in capitalist countries.

Because of the interaction of all these factors international détente in recent years has become a major trend in world development. Our Party, however, by no means considers that all questions bearing on safeguarding peace have been solved and the security of nations effectively ensured.

You, comrades, know very well that the aggressive forces of imperialism have not laid down their weapons. This is evidenced by the arms race which is being whipped up by the forces of imperialism, above all by NATO. Owing to this circumstance, our Party and the Soviet state consider the ending of the arms race to be the key issue today in promoting détente.

In his speech at the Eighteenth Komsomol* Congress Comrade Brezhnev outlined a series of measures which could bring about a cessation of the arms race—in the first place the nuclear arms race—and the subsequent reduction of armaments. In the near future the Special Session of the UN General Assembly on Disarmament will open in New York. We hope it will be able to ensure genuine progress on this essential question. For its part, the Soviet Union will do everything it can toward this end.

The recent visit of Comrade Leonid Brezhnev to the Federal Republic of Germany has undoubtedly helped to consolidate European peace and develop peaceful cooperation between European states. The joint Soviet-West German declaration and other documents adopted during the visit will, we believe, provide a new impulse for furthering détente on our continent.

In the general peace policy of the USSR considerable attention is given to problems relating to the Mediterranean. We are in favor of an early settlement of the Middle East problem, a settlement that would accord with the legitimate interests of all the peoples of this region including the Arab people of Palestine. We are for a just solution of the Cyprus problem, a solution that would ensure the sovereignty and territorial integrity and inviolability of the Republic of Cyprus, and that would reliably uphold the legitimate rights of both communities that make up its population. We are for solving all controversial issues between states situated in the Mediterranean in a peaceful way on the basis of the principles of the UN Charter. Our proposals concerning a mutual withdrawal of ships equipped with nuclear weapons from the Mediterranean still stand. The Soviet Union has declared on

---

* Komsomol—abbreviation for Lenin's Young Communist League, which was founded in the Soviet Republic in 1918. Now it has over 42 million members.

many occasions that it is ready to consider any other ideas relating to an improvement of the situation in the Mediterranean region.

The Soviet Union is for the further all-round development of friendship, cooperation, and good-neighborly relations between our two countries. We consider that there are no obstacles to this and that, on the contrary, there exist all the necessary objective prerequisites for this development. Greece, like the Soviet Union, has signed the Final Act of the Helsinki Conference. Its principles, we believe, form a reliable basis for the development and strengthening of our ties.

Such are the main features of our foreign policy today. It is a policy of peace and cooperation with all nations. Never during the 60 years of its existence has the Soviet Union acted as an aggressive force. We had no plans, nor do we have such plans now, that are hostile to any other country or people. To tell the truth, it is those political forces which today inspire talk about the Soviet military threat that not so long ago took an active part in aggressive actions directed against our country. Knowing this, we of course maintain our defense capability at an appropriate level. We proceed from the principle that socialism and its gains must be reliably protected.

Our Party has always showed revolutionary solidarity with the peoples fighting for freedom and we shall continue to show such solidarity. We have always been and will remain opponents of aggression. This principled policy has always promoted and promotes now a strengthening of peace and consolidation of all forces fighting for a stable peaceful future of mankind.

To the Leninsky Constituency in Kishinev

According to the law on elections to the USSR Supreme Soviet, every candidate on the eve of the election delivers a major speech at a meeting with voters of his or her constituency. Following is an excerpt from the speech made by Konstantin U. Chernenko on February 26, 1979 in Kishinev, the capital of the Moldavian Soviet Socialist Republic, one of the 15 constituent republics located in the southwestern part of the Soviet Union.

Comrades, allow me to dwell on some questions relating to the present-day international situation. First of all, we must say quite frankly that opposition to the policy of détente on the part of reactionary militaristic forces has grown in recent years. They are even trying to go over to counterattacks with the aim of dragging interstate relations back to the grim years of the cold war. They replace peaceful cooperation between states with confrontation, and instead of working for disarmament try to push the world toward stepping up the arms race with all the negative consequences this entails. The pressure exerted by these forces is reflected in the policies of the major Western powers. In the past, too, many of these powers could not be regarded as models of steadfastness in the practical implementation of the principles of peaceful coexistence and good-neighborliness. And today, the vacillations and inconsistencies in their actions and the striving to gain advantage for themselves at the expense of others greatly complicate and prolong the process of promoting mutual understanding and concord between states.

The more estimable and significant are the successes achieved in recent years, despite the schemes of the enemies of peace, in the sphere of international détente, thanks to the tireless efforts of the CPSU Central Committee and the Soviet government, to their initiative and perseverance in the political, economic, ideological, and diplomatic fields. These efforts were based on the reliable defense potential of the Soviet Union, and the Party has always paid and continues to pay close attention to maintaining this potential at the necessary level. This work was carried out jointly and in close coordination with the other socialist countries, our allies and friends.

Peace on earth became more durable. The international position of our country has never been stronger. The efforts of the Soviet Union, its constructive proposals aimed at deepening détente, reducing the armed forces and armaments, cutting down military budgets and thus strengthening international security at a lower level of military confrontation, meet with the approval and support of all progressive forces on our planet. In other words, the impressive Peace Program worked out at the Twenty-fourth and Twenty-fifth Party Congresses is being consistently implemented. For us there is no more sacred cause than that of preserving peace. . . .

The stability of the international position of socialism is best ensured by close unity of the fraternal countries. The Party considers a strengthening of cooperation with these countries to be its prime task. It is pleasant to note that in recent years the ties of friendship and solidarity between the parties and peoples of the socialist countries have been broadened and strengthened. The final victory of the Vietnamese revolution, the formation of a united Socialist Republic of Vietnam, and the completion of the liberation struggle of the people of Laos have led to an extension of the borders of the socialist world and a further consolidation of its influence and authority.

The socialist countries have accumulated valuable experience in coordinating their efforts in the international arena. The meeting of the Political Consultative Committee of the Warsaw Treaty member countries held in Moscow in November 1978 adopted a number of decisions aimed at deepening détente in Europe and throughout the world. At the same time the participants in the meeting warned those circles which tried to gain unilateral advantages and would not hesitate to infringe on the rights of others, that the socialist community would be able to defend its interests and that the intrigues of the enemies of peace would be given a proper rebuff.

Gone forever are the times when imperialism was all-powerful in international relations, when it could insolently and with impunity lord it over the world trampling underfoot the freedom and independence of nations. The power of real socialism, the vigorous foreign policy of the Soviet Union, the international influence of all the fraternal socialist countries, and the growing internationalist solidarity of the Communist and workers' parties are forestalling aggressive imperialist schemes. More favorable conditions are being created for the realization of the age-old dreams of the peoples on different continents fighting for genuine freedom, independence, and deliverance from all forms of oppression. The mighty wave of the national liberation movement is washing away the last seats of colonialism and slavery in the world.

The Soviet Union has always sided and continues to side with the peoples of Angola, Ethiopia, Mozambique, Afghanistan, and other countries which have embarked on the road of building a new life. It was with a feeling of great satisfaction that the Soviet people received the news of the revolution in Kampuchea and the formation of the People's Republic of Kampuchea. The victory of the patriotic forces in Kampuchea has delivered the people from foreign stooges who had turned the life of the people into a real hell.

We sympathize with the Arab peoples who are repulsing the expansionist claims of Israel. There is only one way toward a peaceful settlement in the Middle East: it is the complete withdrawal of Israeli troops from all Arab territories occupied in 1967; recognition of the inalienable rights of the people of Palestine, including their right to self-determination and formation of their own state; and the ensuring of the reliably guaranteed security of all the Middle East states.

Especially tangible are the positive changes in Europe. The Conference on Security and Cooperation in Europe held on the initiative of socialist countries has become an event of historic importance. It has laid the political foundations for peaceful relations on the continent and outlined a broad long-term program of interstate cooperation. In recent years much has been done to develop mutually beneficial ties between socialist and capitalist countries of Europe. The broadening cooperation between the Soviet Union and France and the

Federal Republic of Germany, as well as other West European countries, is a notable contribution to the cause of international détente and the practical implementation of the provisions of the Final Act of the Helsinki Conference.

An improvement of the world situation largely depends on the state of relations between the two major powers—the Soviet Union and the United States. Of late these relations have been at a standstill. And the reason for this is not a lack of fields where U.S.-Soviet cooperation is possible and necessary but an unwillingness on the part of certain U.S. circles to act on the principles of equality. But there is no, nor can there be, other basis for maintaining normal relations between our countries.

This is especially true with respect to disarmament. Here disregard of the principles of equality and equal security will bring no results. As is known, the Soviet Union is ready to take most far-reaching measures in order to curb the arms race and reduce arms stockpiles and the number of troops. For many years already we have been conducting talks with the Americans about limiting offensive strategic arms. It seems that the drafting of the respective agreement is nearing completion. If so, the sides will be able immediately to take up the next projects which will make life in the Soviet Union and the United States and in the rest of the world more tranquil, and which will make it possible to transfer a considerable part of the resources now absorbed by the arms race to constructive undertakings.

Mountains of arms have been accumulated in the world, but there are people who apparently want still more. Every sober-minded person realizes that the Soviet Union and the other socialist countries cannot ignore the accelerated war preparations of the NATO bloc. . . .

The intrigues of reactionary forces demand that we should be vigilant, disciplined, and firm. We declare that the Soviet Union will not leave without a constructive response any proposal that would bring the states closer together in their peaceful efforts. But we say to those who covet what is not theirs: Stop! We are able to stand up for our rights, for the freedom of the peoples of the USSR, and for our friends. The life and peaceful creative labor, the interests of Soviet people are reliably defended by our glorious Armed Forces, which have everything necessary to deal a crushing blow to any aggressor. . . .

At an Awards Ceremony in the City of Frunze

Traditionally, the Soviet Government awards not only the best citizens of the country with orders and medals for acts of courage or expertise in their fields, but also whole cities. Following is an excerpt from a speech Konstantin U. Chernenko delivered on August 15, 1979 in Frunze, the capital of the Kirghiz Soviet Socialist Republic, one of the 15 constituent republics, located in the Asian part of the Soviet Union. The city was presented with the Order of the Red Banner of Labor.

Comrades, since the Twenty-fourth CPSU Congress the broad international public has continued to discuss the peace offensive of the Soviet Union. And indeed, there is no other country in the world which is fighting for peace with such fervor, persistence, and steadfastness as our Motherland. The results of this strenuous work are for all to see: peace has become more stable and secure and cooperation between countries with different social systems is developing more successfully.

As of late, the Treaty on the Limitation of Strategic Offensive Arms* signed in Vienna on June 18 has become a major event of this year.

As you are well aware, the Political Bureau of the CPSU Central Committee, the Presidium of the Supreme Soviet of the USSR, and the Council of Ministers of the USSR attach great importance to this Treaty, which, provided of course it is implemented, would mark a stage of fundamental impor-

---

* SALT-II

tance in the struggle for halting the arms race, a new step towards real disarmament. This is how it is regarded by the Soviet people, and this is how it is regarded throughout the world.

The SALT-II treaty is the result of many years of work, and hard work at that.

Let us recall that only two years ago the American side made attempts actually to cancel the Vladivostok agreement and thus wreck the SALT-II treaty. The Soviet Union had done everything in its power to bring about the drafting and signing of the SALT-II treaty. It would be no exaggeration to say that a tremendous contribution to the drafting of this document of world importance was made by Leonid Ilyich [Brezhnev] personally. This fact is well understood throughout the world.

Certainly, comrades, in our opinion the Treaty on the Limitation of Strategic Arms could have been still better. But we worked not alone but together with the American side and tried to arrive at mutually acceptable solutions. In some respects these solutions are of the nature of a compromise. However, the main thing is that the Treaty provides for a well-thought-out balance of the interests of the two countries.

As for questions which have not yet been solved, we have agreed that the talks should continue. This concerns our bilateral talks with the United States and multilateral talks such as the Vienna talks on the reduction of armaments and armed forces in Central Europe, which have been going on already for a long time. We shall continue to take part in these talks with perseverance so as to obtain positive results. As we see it, the SALT-II treaty provides a good impetus for this.

Nowadays attempts are often being made in the West to present matters in such a way as to suggest that the Soviet Union is almost the only side that has a stake in the Treaty and is for this reason especially concerned about its future, and in particular about its ratification.

Naturally, we would like to see this Treaty ratified and put into force. But we wish this not at all because our country allegedly has a greater stake in it than any other country. We are convinced that both the USSR and the U.S. are equally interested in the SALT-II treaty, in its complete and unconditional implementation. All the nations, all those who want to prevent a nuclear war, are interested in the success of this

Treaty. This belief arises from our conviction that there is no alternative to a peace policy, that in our time it is the only sensible policy.

It goes without saying that we are prepared to carry out all the provisions of the Treaty signed in Vienna, and exactly as they are formulated. This was quite definitely underlined in Vienna by Leonid Ilyich [Brezhnev]. We consider it inadmissible to call in question any part of the Treaty under this or that pretext. That is how we approach the matter and we expect the same approach from the American side.

The SALT-II treaty has another important aspect. You are aware, comrades, that Soviet-U.S. relations have of late been developing unevenly. Brief periods of their more or less intensive development were followed by deteriorations and artificial complications. The blame for this does not lie with the Soviet Union. Meanwhile, all the nations of the world felt themselves the losers, for it is no secret that the entire international climate greatly depends on the development of Soviet-U.S. relations.

As we see it, the SALT-II treaty provides an opportunity for putting Soviet-U.S. relations on a path of more even, carefully weighed and balanced development based on the principles of peaceful coexistence and mutually advantageous cooperation, respect for each other's sovereignty, and non-interference in each other's internal affairs. We believe that this serves the interests of the whole world.

To be brief, we believe that the Vienna meeting could provide an impetus for taking new important steps towards deepening détente, toward combining political détente with military détente, and toward greatly expanding peaceful co-operation.

In particular, the favorable effect of this Treaty will probably be felt in Europe. There has been no war in this important part of the world for 34 years already. Moreover, in West European countries there are now in fact no influential political circles which would consider it possible, with the existing correlation of forces, to adhere to a course of crushing the socialist world by military means.

Peace in Europe is at times regarded as something quite usual, something which goes without saying. Probably there are those who think that after the cold war was replaced by détente the peaceful situation in Europe would be preserved automatically in the future. This is far from being the case. Persistent day-to-day efforts are required to consolidate and develop détente in Europe. This task is of constant concern to Leonid Ilyich Brezhnev, the whole Political Bureau, the Soviet government, to our diplomatic corps.

As you will recall, we have put forward a number of new important proposals aimed at a further improvement of the situation in Europe. One of them, in particular, calls for the conclusion of a nonaggression treaty among the participants in the Helsinki European Conference. Among the other major initiatives put forward were those envisaging an extension of military confidence-building measures. These proposals were supported and further developed at the meeting of the Committee of Foreign Ministers of the Warsaw Treaty member countries.

In the struggle for peace we act together with the fraternal socialist countries; together we are carrying out large-scale work and are getting positive results. Friendship and cooperation among socialist countries are growing and being further consolidated. This is evidenced by the recent visit of the Soviet Party and government delegation headed by Leonid Ilyich to Hungary. While in that country the Soviet delegation had an opportunity once again to feel the warm friendship and genuine cordial relations between our peoples.

The meetings and talks Leonid Ilyich recently had with Party and government leaders of socialist countries have served to deepen and enrich our ties with fraternal countries. The talks in the Crimea concerned not only current matters but also important problems pertaining to the future of the socialist world. What is discussed at such meetings is later reflected in the decisions of Party congresses, in joint moves in the international arena, and in the coordination of five-year plans. Naturally, the importance of such work cannot be overestimated.

Quite recently we celebrated the thirtieth anniversary of the Council for Mutual Economic Assistance. Together we have carried out work of tremendous importance in these 30 years. Today the countries, members of the Council for Mutual Economic Assistance, which account for ten percent of the world population, produce a quarter of the world national income and a third of world industrial and agricultural output. The relations between our countries, which are relations of fraternal friendship and mutual assistance, are a prototype of the future relations between all countries and nations on our planet.

We are of course well aware that it is not an easy and simple task to develop and strengthen détente. The cause of détente has its opponents, and they are strong opponents indeed. First of all, there are the NATO circles. Even now, after the SALT-II treaty has been signed, the NATO military leaders have only one thing on their mind—somehow to add new weapon systems to their already existing stockpiles of nuclear-missile weapons. To camouflage these plans they repeatedly use the myth about the Soviet military threat. So our common struggle, the struggle we wage together with the socialist countries, for the continuation and deepening of détente, will require still greater efforts on our part.

The situation in many regions of the world is far from simple. In this connection I cannot help mentioning the attempts of the forces of reaction and imperialism to interfere in the internal affairs of a country which is our neighbor—democratic Afghanistan. Those forces spare no efforts to deprive the Afghan people of their revolutionary gains and to restore feudal order there. We are confident that the plans of reactionaries are doomed to failure.

At the Soviet-Bulgarian Friendship Meeting

The exchange of delegations of high-ranking Communist Party and government representatives plays an important part in strengthening all-round cooperation and expanding fraternal contacts between socialist countries. Following is the speech delivered by Konstantin Chernenko on December 5, 1979 during an official visit of the Soviet delegation to the People's Republic of Bulgaria. The speech was delivered at a factory for telephone and telegraph apparatus in Sofia.

Dear Comrades, in paying a good deal of attention to the questions of the building of communism, the development of relations with fraternal socialist countries, and the all-round consolidation of the socialist community, the CPSU with its allies and friends is actively and consistently working to ensure peace on earth. Among the many important and far from easy international problems, the tasks of making détente more of a reality, and fighting against the arms race and for disarmament, are central to world politics today.

Today's world situation, as it is taking shape on the threshold of the 1980s, has forced humanity to make a choice: either to get rid of the mountains of weapons which block the path to a lasting peace, or to wander through the maze of military confrontation and risk plunging into the abyss any moment. We the socialist countries say: Our system has no need of war, we threaten no one. We link our future with peaceful cooperation among states and nations, with the complete eradication of violence from international relations. If all this depended on the socialist countries alone, then there is no doubt that the people of our planet would not experience the threat of war, the fear of being hostages in the nuclear missile manipulations of the imperialist forces.

In reality the world, however, is different. The aggressive forces have not laid down their weapons. Their influence on the policies of the imperialist states and those in alliance with them cannot be underestimated. It is still great.

The fierce struggle between the supporters and opponents of détente was a permanent feature of the 1970s, a decade which is almost history. In this struggle, victory was on the side of reason, on the side of the world's peace-loving forces. The ideas of détente gained the upper hand. The Soviet Union and other socialist countries succeeded in drawing broad sections of the world public to the side of the policy of peace and cooperation and in securing the understanding of the governments of many states.

One of the most important achievements of the 1970s is the signing by the Soviet Union and the United States of a new Treaty on the Limitation of Strategic Offensive Arms— SALT-II. It is intended to stabilize the international situation, to create prerequisites for new and wider measures in the task of genuine disarmament. That is why the nations expect this Treaty to be put into effect without delay.

But the world situation remains complicated. One must, for the time being, regard as inevitable the instability of the policies of the Western countries and the striking incompatibility between their noble declarations and their practical steps.

Less than two months ago, comrade Leonid Brezhnev put forward new peace initiatives in Berlin. Their aim is to promote military détente and arms limitation on the European continent.

But the proposals to conduct talks on these questions, the example of good will which the Soviet Union has shown, have not been met with a positive response from the NATO states. Before sitting down at the negotiating table, they say, the North Atlantic bloc must make a decision to produce and deploy in Western Europe qualitatively new systems of American nuclear missiles. But this would mean undermining the chances of achieving positive results at the talks.

The implication of NATO's venture is clear—to achieve military superiority over the socialist countries in Europe. And no secret is made of this. I want to say clearly: Such plans are doomed to failure. Anyone who intends to talk to us from a "position of strength" is, as the past has shown more than once, making a serious miscalculation.

The socialist countries will not permit themselves to be pushed off their chosen course. "The policy of détente—and everyone knows how much socialist countries have done to make it a success," comrade Leonid Brezhnev said in Berlin, "has given rise to great hopes. It is essential that they be justified. We are in favor of freeing the 1980s from a 'war of nerves,' from suspicion and fear, and, most important of all, from the arms race.

"Genuine political courage does not consist in a thirst for rivalry and confrontation, but in the ability to pursue the policy of peace and good-neighborliness without vacillation and deviation."

This is how the Soviet Union, People's Republic of Bulgaria, and other countries of the socialist community act and will continue to act. In all international affairs we act together, defending the interests of peace, the right of the nations to free, independent development, against any intrigues of imperialism and manifestations of hegemony-seeking. This is a correct policy, answering the interests of all nations. We have pursued and will continue to pursue it undeviatingly!

To the Voters of the Kuibyshev Constituency in Moscow

The following is an excerpt from the speech made by Konstantin U. Chernenko on February 15, 1980 in one of the districts of Moscow during the election campaign for the USSR Supreme Soviet, the Soviet legislature. The speaker reported to his voters on various aspects of the international situation and Soviet foreign policy.

As you know, today some people in the West are cynically calculating how much the food situation in the Soviet Union will worsen as a result of the United States' refusal to sell us grain. In this way they want to bring pressure of a kind to bear on the Soviet Union and even, as some Western Sovietologists declare, to make our country alter the course of its foreign policy. Naturally, all these attempts are futile. A proper answer to all these politicians who have lost all sense of proportion and reality was given by Leonid Brezhnev who said:

> Of course, these actions by the U.S. administration will not inflict on us the damage their initiators obviously hope for. The cynical estimates concerning the "worsening" of the food situation in the Soviet Union as a result of the U.S. refusal to sell us grain are based on ridiculous notions about our economic potential. The Soviet people have sufficient resources to live and work with calm, to fulfill their plans and raise living standards.

. . . Comrades, all our work and all our aspirations are directed toward ensuring stable peace and prosperity for the

Soviet people and our socialist state. To wish for peace for yourself means to wish for peace for your allies and friends as well, for your partners with whom you have treaties and agreements. To work for progress for Soviet people means to recognize the right of other peoples to well-being and progress and to be ready to take into consideration their legitimate interests.

The experience of the 1970s has proved that there is no way, nor can there be any way, to reliable and durable peace other than the consistent implementation of the principles of peaceful coexistence of states with different social systems irrespective of their size and strength. There is no question for our Party and state about what to choose in our foreign policy. We made our choice long ago in favor of détente and cooperation because we are firmly convinced that there is no reasonable alternative to it. The Soviet Union has not budged an inch from this course.

As you are aware, comrades, the international situation has recently become considerably more complicated. Reactionary imperialist forces are intent on marking the beginning of the new decade in the life of mankind with fierce attacks on the very foundations of peaceful coexistence. The deep-going changes that are now taking place on our planet are not to their liking. They are frightened by the consolidation of the positions of socialism, the development of the social and national liberation movement, and the strengthening of the independence of states. The forces of reaction are searching for ways to influence the course of events and to turn the tide of this development. To achieve this they provoke conflicts, heighten tension, and rattle the saber.

This is not the first time that peoples have encountered attempts by the exploiting classes to stop the onward march of history. This is not the first time that imperialism has tried to style itself the judge of the destinies of other peoples. Nothing came of these attempts earlier, nothing will come of them now. Mankind will further develop according to its own laws, and not according to those which Washington and some other imperialist centers would like to impose on it.

Recent years have seen the Leninist foreign policy of the CPSU and the Soviet state win significant successes. They testify to the realistic nature of the Peace Program worked out by the Twenty-fourth and Twenty-fifth CPSU Congresses and prove that the tasks it set were justified.

The socialist community has become the most dynamic and stable force favorably influencing all world events.

The appearance of a group of new states which have chosen the socialist path of development is an event of historic importance. United socialist Vietnam is developing successfully. Laos has declared its adherence to socialist ideals.

The Kampuchean people have overthrown the fanatical regime of Maoist puppets. We were recently glad to welcome to the Soviet Union the leaders of reborn Kampuchea.

Anti-imperialist revolutions have been victorious in Ethiopia, Angola, Mozambique, and Afghanistan. The Shah's tyranny has been done away with in Iran. The people of Nicaragua have thrown off the bloody and corrupt dictatorship.

On the whole, there have been marked positive changes in the planet's political climate. Détente has struck deep roots. People understand more clearly the necessity and possibility of curbing the arms race and setting to real disarmament. The signing in June 1979 of the Soviet-American SALT-II treaty would have opened the way to further serious steps in this field, so important for the destiny of the world if, naturally, the Treaty had been ratified and a start had been made on translating it into life.

This, however, was precisely what least of all suited certain circles in the U.S. and several other NATO countries, as well as the Peking leadership. These circles have laid plans in quite a different direction. They needed the arms race at all costs because all their plans were tied up, not with achieving accord between states and strengthening international security, but with creating tension in the world.

It thus transpires that, while signing the SALT-II treaty, i.e., the obligation not to strive for military superiority, with one hand, the U.S. administration was increasing the pressure of its other hand on all levers in an attempt to make its West European partners agree to new American nuclear missiles and to plunge the world deeper into the whirlpool of the arms race. For this purpose President Carter announced the introduction of a five-year militarist program to revive and to back with the force of arms U.S. claims to the "leading role" in the world, the policy of barefaced hegemonism.

In his recent replies to a *Pravda* correspondent, Leonid Brezhnev provided a clear-cut Marxist-Leninist analysis of the international situation and gave a principled appraisal of the aggressive imperialist circles' intrigues.

The U.S. administration and the Western propaganda machine at its service claim that the Americans have taken a hard line in response to the mythical "Soviet military threat" and the no less mythical "Soviet expansionism" in Africa, Latin America, and the Middle East. The favorite theme concerns Soviet military assistance to Afghanistan, which has allegedly violated the strategic balance in a region where according to American leaders' statements the U.S. has "vital interests."

All these and similar allegations are false from beginning to end. There is not a grain of truth in statements that the Soviet Union is threatening somebody. Talk about Soviet plans to appropriate natural riches, oil, and raw materials in the Middle East and to endanger international sea communications is ill-intentioned and false. Carter and his advisers have not invented anything new resorting to these accusations. They are only repeating the absurd fabrications of the anti-Sovieteers of earlier times. There have been many who have slandered our country and the Leninist Communist Party, but truth has always won in the end.

In recent statements President Carter has cynically admitted that from his very first days in office he made the buildup of U.S. military potential the cornerstone of his policy. According to him, he considers weapons to be the American trump card, the decisive argument backing up Washington's desire to dictate its will to those countries and even whole regions on which for different reasons—political, military, or economic—the American imperialist circles have their eye. Back in May 1978, pressed by the United States, the NATO bloc adopted a decision binding its members annually to increase their military budgets up to the year 2000.

What has Afghanistan to do with all this? The Afghan events, about which Western propaganda is making so much noise now, did not exist when the U.S. began to create the notorious rapid deployment force, i.e., forces of military intervention, to militarize the Indian Ocean and to search for ways of military penetration into the Persian Gulf, which resulted finally in the concentration in this region of the biggest American military and naval grouping. This grouping is still in close proximity to the Iranian and other Muslim countries' coastlines, keeping its guns trained on them.

"If there had been no Afghanistan," stressed Leonid Brezhnev, "certain circles in the United States and NATO would surely have found another pretext for aggravating the world situation." Indeed, they made no secret of their intentions. Suffice it to recall the "crisis" artificially created over the alleged presence in Cuba of a Soviet army unit, or the clamor about alleged Soviet superiority in medium-range weapons in Europe, or the brazen threats of the U.S. to deal with Iran if the latter did not bow down to Washington's will.

The influential circles in the U.S. needed tension, and they and nobody else have created this tension. President Carter personally needs tension because he hopes to surge to victory over his rivals in the presidential campaign on a wave of chauvinism and anticommunist hysteria. Elections are each country's internal affair, but President Carter is engaged in throwing relations between states years back and dragging the world into the abyss of the cold war, an even more adventuristic scheme than some of his predecessors entertained.

It is worthwhile to note who is praising Carter for his "hard-line" policies. They are dictatorial regimes of different kinds which have been created and exist with Washington's backing, and the revanchist rabble dreaming about the revision of the results of the Second World War. They are also the present Chinese leaders who have taken the course of open collaboration with imperialism and are striving to gain its military support.

Life will put everything in its place. It will put in their place those in the United States and other countries who would like to take upon themselves the thankless task of teaching others how to live. There is no doubt that Carter and others will fail in their attempts to change the world and the peoples inhabiting it to their liking. Times are now not what they were, nor is the alignment of forces in the world.

It is important to be calm and sober-minded in the present complex situation. The aggressive forces are eager to make the Soviet Union take a hard line in response. The Soviet Union can stand up for its interests and the interests of its friends in the correct way—convincingly and resolutely. Nobody should entertain any doubts on this score, but neither in the future will we deviate from the general course aimed at friendship and peace among nations and at the elimination of wars from the life of mankind, the course handed down to us by Lenin. Today we repeat again that we link our hopes and our plans not with the subjugation of other peoples, but with cooperation with them, with the solution of difficult problems arising between states through honest and equitable negotiations.

The 1970s have left mankind a good inheritance. They have also given us instructive experience in how to conduct international affairs. On the constructive policies of all governments, and on these policies alone, depends whether use will be made of the objective possibilities to preserve and augment the already existing achievements.

At an Awards Ceremony in the City of Chelyabinsk

Chelyabinsk, a large industrial center in the Urals, has won nationwide recognition for its outstanding economic performance during the war with Nazi Germany and later in the postwar period. The Order of Lenin is the highest award of the Soviet Government, and Konstantin U. Chernenko presented it to the city in a special ceremony on May 29,1980.

You know, comrades, that today some people across the ocean are attempting to prove the opposite, performing new variations on the old theme of applying "economic sanctions" against the Soviet Union. I think it would be appropriate here to recall what Lenin said:

> We have been threatened often enough, and with much more serious threats than those uttered by the merchant who intends to slam the door. . . . And if you gentlemen, who represent the bourgeois governments, care to amuse yourselves . . . and to overload your cables and radio stations with messages announcing to the whole world: "We shall put Russia to the test," we shall see who comes off best. We have already been put to the test, not to the test of words, not to the test of trade, not to the test of money, but the test of the bludgeon.

Of course we cannot compel foreign "strategists" to study the works of Lenin. But once again it is apparently necessary to remind some people of the lessons of history. Such lessons, by the way, have been given by the workers of Chelyabinsk.

For example, certain Western firms attempted to put us into a difficult position at one point, by suddenly refusing to sell large-diameter steel pipes. So then the workers at Chelyabinsk's pipe-making factory had their say. In record time they mastered the production of our own pipes, thereby showing the capitalists what Soviet workers of the Urals are capable of.

It must be said that today some people apparently not only do not wish to reckon with the lessons of history but even attempt to turn the clock back. At the beginning of a new decade the world situation has become significantly complex.

They often assert in the West that the aggravation of the world situation has been caused by events in Afghanistan or Iran. This is not true. It was not today or yesterday that the forces of imperialism, and above all the United States, adopted a line which is hostile towards peace.

At a conference of the Political Consultative Committee of the Warsaw Treaty member-states in May this year, a consistent analysis was made of the contemporary international situation, and it was demonstrated how directly responsible the aggressive circles of the imperialist powers are for the growing threat to peace and the independence of nations. The complication of the situation at the present time is a direct consequence of the imperialist policy of force, confrontation, and hegemony. Imperialism attempts to restore military superiority over the socialist countries and to bring extensive areas of the world under its control.

Does not the program for a large-scale military build up, intended for the next 20 years, which was adopted by NATO two years ago, testify to this? Did not the leaders of the NATO bloc make this their aim when, in response to our proposal for reducing the threat of war in Europe, they took the decision to deploy new U.S. nuclear medium-range missiles aimed against the Soviet Union? And what about the sabotaging of the ratification of the SALT-II treaty? The enemies of détente, as we can see, are not idle.

The more limited imperialism's chance to subordinate other nations and peoples to its hegemony, to plunder their natural resources without hindrance, the more violent is the reaction of the forces of imperialism, particularly the United States of America.

Faced with a very serious crisis situation, the most aggressive forces in the United States are attempting, by saber-rattling and by introducing economic sanctions, to impose their will on other countries.

The Carter administration's decision to break off diplomatic relations with Iran, to impose an economic blockade on it, and to deploy in the Persian Gulf massive U.S. naval forces, is an undisguised escalation of blackmail, pressure, and tension in the Middle East.

Let's turn to Afghanistan. If our military contingent had not entered the country according to a request by the Afghan government then forces hostile to peace would have turned the country into a base, from which they would have threatened the Soviet Union's southern borders and drowned the Afghan revolution in blood. Would this have strengthened détente? Of course not. A few days ago the Afghan government came forward with an initiative envisaging a political settlement of the situation there. We support these proposals. . . .

Iran, Afghanistan, the Middle East, the Indian Ocean — all these are links in one chain, a chain which is leading to a growing threat of war for all states and peoples. The Chinese leaders, by taking the path of directly siding with imperialism, are more and more actively joining forces with those who are dragging the world toward a dangerous course of events.

Remaining true to its wolfish nature and wolfish habits, striving, as the famous Russian writer Ivan Krylov said in his well-known fable, "To give the deed the sense and form of legality," imperialism seeks any pretext to justify its expansionist plans, adventurist "doctrines," and the whipping up of a militarist hysteria. Having adopted methods of propaganda inherited from Goebbels, the new advocates of the "position of strength" policy play up to the utmost the myth about the "Soviet military threat."

The anti-Soviet hysteria whipped up by Carter and his colleagues recently is unprecedented in its maliciousness. There is hardly a fabrication that they have not used.

Leonid Brezhnev had this to say: "We oppose the 'doctrine' of war hysteria and a feverish arms race with the doctrine of a consistent struggle for peace and security in the world. We are faithful to the Peace Program put forward by the Twenty-fourth and Twenty-fifth Congresses of our Party."

The Soviet Union, as before, consistently comes forward for strengthening détente, reducing armaments, and for rapprochement and mutual understanding between nations. Our Leninist foreign policy is close to the hearts and clear to all who need and value peace, who are fighting for the freedom and independence of the nations, and for social progress.

All the member-countries of the Warsaw Treaty stand faithfully with the Soviet Union in guarding peace and socialism. In its 25 years of existence this organization has emerged and acts as a reliable shield to defend socialist achievements, as a powerful factor in the common struggle for peace and international security, and as a source of the most important peace initiatives.

A concise program of moves for preserving peace was put forward in the declaration and statement unanimously adopted by the Political Consultative Committee at its conference in Warsaw. The program contains new constructive proposals aimed at further developing détente on the European continent, curbing the arms race, and generally improving the political climate in the world.

In response to the intrigues of the forces of imperialism the Soviet people close their ranks still more tightly around the Communist Party and its Central Committee and redouble their efforts in the name of strengthening the economic and defensive might of their beloved Motherland.

Trust and Cooperation among Peoples

The following is the text of an article by Konstantin U. Chernenko printed in the Soviet monthly journal International Affairs *(no. 8, August 1980). The article emphasizes that the Helsinki Conference, concluded on August 1, 1975 with the signing of the Final Act by the 33 European countries, the United States, and Canada, had an important impact on making the political situation in Europe and the whole world healthier.*

As a member of the Soviet delegation at the Conference in Helsinki I particularly feel the great positive impact its decisions have on normalizing international relations, strengthening mutual understanding, and spreading the spirit of détente. During the past five years the world nations saw for themselves that it is possible to achieve accord and understanding between states with different systems on complex foreign policy issues even in difficult conditions; that it is possible to lessen and even remove mutual suspicion through contacts and talks; to expand trust by developing multifaceted cooperation; that it is possible to improve substantially and ease the situation in Europe; and thereby to consolidate international security and peace.

The five years since the Conference have shown that the realization of the provisions of the Final Act signed in Helsinki, this charter of European peace and security and a long-term program for cooperation between states and peoples, has become a major direction in European political affairs. It has introduced new constructive elements into international relations, filling them with new content and meaning. Bilateral and multilateral contacts and consultations between governments have noticeably expanded and become more frequent in Europe; many agreements have been concluded that are in line with the spirit of the Helsinki accords and are directed at strengthening security in Europe and developing the cooperation of states in the economy, science and technology, in environmental protection, and also in humanitarian fields. The great importance of efforts to fulfill the provisions of the Final Act for making the principles of peaceful coexistence a rule of international intercourse has been proved in practice. . . .

By its actions the Soviet Union has demonstrated its adherence to the principles elaborated in Helsinki. The policy of consistent implementation of the accords reached at the European Conference is clearly reflected in many documents of the CPSU Central Committee and the Soviet government, and in their practical activities.

In its documents the Twenty-fifth CPSU Congress in 1976 put on record the firm resolve of the CPSU and the Soviet government to fulfill the "code of rules of détente" formulated in the Final Act. The Program of Further Struggle for Peace and International Cooperation and for the Freedom and Independence of the Peoples sets the task of working "vigorously for the full implementation of the Final Act of the European Conference, and for greater peaceful cooperation in Europe."

The inclusion in the new 1977 Constitution of the USSR of fundamental principles defining the nature of the Leninist policy of peace and international cooperation graphically showed the Soviet Union's sincere attitude to the cause of détente and security in the world. Leonid Brezhnev said:

> By including in the new Constitution a special chapter formalizing the peaceful character of the foreign policy of the Soviet Union, our people have once again stressed their determination to follow the Leninist course of peace, the course of ridding humanity of the horrors of war, of the material hardships and mortal dangers implicit in the arms race. This chapter contains clauses corresponding to the fundamental obligations that the Soviet Union has undertaken as a participant in vital international agreements, including the Final Act of the Helsinki Conference. Indisputably, this imparts additional weight to the efforts

that are being made in the world for a further normalization of the international situation, for the development of détente.

During numerous meetings, conferences, and talks the leaders of the CPSU and government had with the heads of foreign states and governments in the last five years, the Soviet side invariably stressed the need consistently to implement all the provisions of the Final Act of the Helsinki Conference, and made proposals on the development of bilateral and multilateral cooperation in the fields covered by this Act. . . .

Following the European Conference the Soviet Union has signed more than 30 agreements and programs in the field of economic cooperation with France, the FRG, Italy, Finland, Denmark, Portugal, and other countries. A number of agreements on cultural, scientific, technical, and tourist exchanges have also been concluded with countries participating in the Conference.

The fundamental principles of international relations recorded in the Final Act have become important foreign policy guidelines for other countries of the socialist community as well.

The initiative of socialist countries in proposing in 1976 to conclude an agreement on the basic principles governing relations between the CMEA and the EEC was highly assessed in Europe. This proposal, made in the spirit of Helsinki, has led to negotiations between the two organizations which are going on.

The notion of "post-Helsinki Europe" has come into being during these years. Basically, it characterizes the established system of fruitful ties and contacts between the states of the continent, the new political and other possibilities for the development of good-neighborly, equitable, and mutually advantageous relations in all fields and, moreover, not only in what is called "big-time politics" but also in the sphere of improving the well-being of people, providing them with work and opportunities for education, cultural development, and so on.

The period that has passed since the European Conference shows that the work started in Helsinki has proved its tremendous political and practical usefulness and viability. It is no longer possible to reject or ignore it. It is for good reason that the thesis that there is no reasonable alternative to the policy of détente has been acknowledged throughout Europe. The experience accumulated since the Conference shows that if states do intend to observe the accords reached in Helsinki and develop good-neighborly relations, then the possibility appears of reaching important international agreements on the expansion of cooperation, maintenance of security, and reduction of armaments.

At the same time, the past few years have confirmed that each step toward strengthening international security and developing détente requires resolute struggle against the imperialist policy of power and diktat, confrontation and unleashing of conflicts, the arms race and interference in internal affairs. This policy made itself felt more than once and had a particularly adverse effect on restraining the arms race. In their efforts to consolidate international détente and lessen the level of military confrontation in Europe, the socialist countries have invariably raised the question of the need to supplement political détente with détente in the military sphere. In accordance with the spirit and letter of the Final Act, they repeatedly came out with initiatives and proposals to this effect. But most of them encountered reluctance on the part of the United States and its NATO allies to take practical steps in these directions.

Thus in November 1978, the Warsaw Treaty participants* outlined in the Moscow Declaration a broad program of measures aimed at introducing a change in relations between states toward building trust and developing all-round cooperation, limiting the arms race and achieving disarmament, promoting in this way military détente in Europe. How did the West respond to this? It chose to avoid giving an answer to the proposal for all participants in the European Conference to conclude a treaty under which they would undertake not to be the first to use either nuclear or conventional weapons against each other, to observe in Europe the principle of nonuse of force or threat of force. Nor was there an answer to the proposal of socialist countries not to expand membership of the Warsaw Treaty and NATO, to reduce military budgets,

---

* The Political Consultative Committee of the member states of the Warsaw Treaty Organization held a meeting on November 22–23, 1978 in Moscow.

and so on. It was already at that time that the NATO countries had geared themselves to a new stage in the arms race which was started by the adoption in the spring of 1978 of the unprecedented long-term program for building up and modernizing the bloc's armaments.

In May 1979, the Committee of Foreign Ministers of the Warsaw Treaty countries* came forward with a new initiative aimed at ensuring security in Europe. It proposed to convene a European conference at a political level which, along with questions of military détente and disarmament on the European continent, would discuss confidence building measures between states. And again the NATO countries did not give a clear answer.

In December 1979, the Committee of Foreign Ministers again called for considering military détente and disarmament in Europe the key issue in the efforts to consolidate European peace and security. It drew attention to the existence in NATO of dangerous plans for further intensifying the arms race in Europe and proposed to commence, without delay, talks on medium-range nuclear weapons in accordance with the proposals outlined in Leonid Brezhnev's speech in Berlin on October 6, 1979. But once more the West neglected this opportunity for turning developments in Europe towards strengthening détente on the basis of measures aimed at lessening the level of armaments and building confidence. Instead, NATO adopted a plan of deploying in Western Europe new American medium-range missiles, one which the United States stubbornly insisted on.

The meeting of the Political Consultative Committee of the Warsaw Treaty member states in May 1980 was a fresh demonstration of the firm adherence of the socialist countries to the policy of peaceful coexistence and relaxation of tension and of their loyalty to the Helsinki principles and accords. They again called on all peace-loving countries and peoples to concentrate their efforts on the central problem of our time—the problem of military détente and disarmament, including in Europe. The Warsaw Declaration sets forth a detailed program of actions which, if implemented, will stop the sliding of Europe, and the world as a whole, down to the

---

* A meeting of the Foreign Ministers Committee of the Warsaw Treaty member states was held on May 14, 1979 in Budapest.

danger line. In Warsaw, the socialist countries made a major proposal—to conduct shortly afterwards a summit meeting of the leaders of states of all areas of the world to discuss questions of eliminating seats of international tension and preventing war.

Already in the Moscow Declaration of 1978 the socialist countries pointed to the invigorated activities of the forces of imperialism and reaction, to their intensified attempts to dominate independent states and peoples, and to their crude interference in the internal affairs of other states. Decisions by NATO countries concerning the adoption of the long-term program for building up and modernizing armaments almost up to the end of the century or the deployment of new American missiles in Western Europe demonstrate the intention of certain quarters in the West to achieve military superiority over the socialist countries and the desire to dictate to them, which blatantly contradicts the very essence of the Helsinki accords.

At attempt is being made to justify the aggressiveness that is gaining the upper hand in NATO's policy by the alleged "Soviet threat" to the West. This myth has long been disproved by world development. So without going into details it should only be said that it is being shamelessly used by imperialist propaganda to cover up the truly peace endangering actions by the American and NATO military in Europe and beyond.

Resorting to the subversive maneuvers against the Helsinki accords imperialist reactionaries not only disregard the agreed upon principles of relations between states, but also try to distort the provisions of the Final Act and place them at the service of their selfish interests. These tactics are particularly evident in the hypocritical attempts of the Washington administration to pose as a "protector of human rights" in the socialist countries. Just as obvious is the entire groundlessness of charges against the socialist countries of supposed "violations" of the rights of their citizens and of claims to the role of champions of human rights and freedoms by the ruling circles of the state where the flouting of the political, economic, and social rights of millions of people has become a daily norm of life. It is not surprising, therefore, that the attempt by the United States to turn the Belgrade meeting (October 1977–March 1978) of the states that had participated in the European Conference into a venue for "condemning" socialist countries was frustrated. The American delegation's policy of confrontation and "psychological warfare," of distorting the essence of the Helsinki accords, did not and could not bring it success. The objective interest of European countries in cooperation and peace prevailed in Belgrade.

Washington's foreign policy during most of the post-Helsinki period has been marked by an openly militaristic course and attempts to speak with the USSR in the language of cold war. The Carter administration has not stopped short of violating the political, trade, economic, and other treaties and agreements signed by the United States, thereby breaking the principle of good faith in fulfilling obligations under international law recorded in the United Nations Charter and the Final Act of the European Conference. It appears that it intends to undermine the process of détente, good-neighborliness and mutual understanding which has been gaining momentum after Helsinki, and to scale down the cooperation which has not always been distinguished for genuine reciprocity on the part of the West. Washington must have seen détente as an obstacle to its aggressive plans, to the whipping up of militaristic hysteria, and to interference in the internal affairs of other states.

The events in Afghanistan were perceived and used in the United States as a pretext for departure from the policy of détente, for demonstratively placing the emphasis on the position-of-strength policy, and for reviving the cold war spirit.

Life in Afghanistan is now gradually returning to normal. Large bands of counterrevolutionaries have been routed and the interventionists have suffered a serious defeat. In this situation the Soviet Union adopted the decision to withdraw some units of its military contingent from Afghanistan. The USSR is doing this on agreement with the Afghan government and its leader, Babrak Karmal. It goes without saying that in the future too the Soviet Union will help Afghanistan build its new life and protect the gains of the April Revolution.

It was long before the Afghan events that the main trends in the present American administration's "new" course began to form. They embrace the NATO decision on the 15-year program for building up the bloc's armaments and on the annual increase of military spending during this period; the decision of the United States on the five-year program of developing new weapon systems; the decision on the deployment of new American nuclear missile weapons in Europe fraught with a great danger to the continent; the indefinite procrastination of the SALT-II treaty ratification; rapprochement with Peking on an anti-Soviet basis; and last but not least, the mounting campaign of anti-Soviet hysteria. So today the prime cause of the worsening of the international situation lies in the United States.

The present Washington administration's hegemonistic ambitions were openly outlined in Carter's State of the Union message to Congress in January 1980, in his speech in Philadelphia in May, and in other statements. They virtually announce imperialism's claim to world domination, to the attainment of military superiority, and to the "right" to dictate its will to other states. They proclaim the course for confrontation, for renouncing the achievements of political détente, whose basic principles were recorded in the Final Act, and set forth the concept of reliance on military power as the principal means of reaching the foreign policy aims of the United States.

Washington is trying to pursue a hostile and even provocative policy toward not only the USSR but also other states, which is hardly compatible with normal relations between states. Such is the policy of interference, pressure, brute force, and violation of sovereignty that the United States is pursuing in Iran, shamelessly exploiting the "hostage problem" which it itself has provoked. Such are the armed aggressions against the Democratic Republic of Afghanistan, orchestrated by the United States, and provocations against the Republic of Cuba. Such is the total disregard for the rights of the Arab people of Palestine and the utmost support for the Israeli aggressors. Finally, such is the policy of imperialist pressure on countries of the Persian Gulf and the Indian Ocean, exerted by means of a powerful military fist which has been created there, and also the old and new military bases.

Analyzing dangerous consequences of the adventuristic elements inherent in the present U.S. foreign policy course for the whole world, Leonid Brezhnev said that "Washington's arbitrary arrogation of a 'right' to 'reward' or to 'punish' at will independent sovereign states raises a question of principle. By such actions the U.S. government is actually striking a blow at the entire system of relations between states based on international law." There is no doubt that the present U.S.

policy flagrantly contradicts the principles and provisions of the Final Act of the European Conference that the United States has signed among other countries. Should one be surprised after this that an appeal to the Carter administration to unilaterally "cancel" U.S. participation in the Helsinki accords appeared in the *New York Times* late in May?

It should be noted that the European allies of the United States, though forced by "Atlantic solidarity" to follow their senior NATO partner, are showing an interest, to a greater or lesser extent, in preserving the policy of détente which has produced especially tangible results in Europe. They understand that there is no need to subordinate the long-term interests of European states to the American administration's whims or emotional outbursts, to its considerations of instant advantage or election campaigning. The maintenance and strengthening of détente on the European continent largely depend on how carefully all states that took part in the European Conference treat the positive experience accumulated in Europe during the past decade and on how consistently they implement all the principles and provisions of the Final Act.

The Soviet Union and the other socialist states are determined to do everything they can not only to preserve all the positive experience that has been accumulated during the past decade, including after the Conference in Helsinki, but also to multiply the gains of détente. In the Warsaw Declaration they denounced attempts to undermine détente, to obstruct the development of cooperation between states. They resolutely came out against the revival of an atmosphere of hostility and mistrust on the European continent. For the European peoples, who from their own experience know how profoundly détente accords with their interests, the maintenance of détente and the development of equitable cooperation are vitally important, just as they are for all the peoples of the world. It is essential that the present political, economic, scientific, technological, and other peaceful ties between the participants in the European Conference further develop, and that the exchange of views, ideas, and considerations on pressing European and world problems between them continue within the framework of political contacts and consultations. . . .

In November 1980, a follow-up meeting of the participant states in the European Conference is to be held in Madrid. The socialist countries consider it imperative to prepare for the meeting thoroughly and to create an atmosphere of trust and mutual understanding. For this reason they proposed to intensify the exchange of views on a bilateral and multilateral basis so that before the start of the meeting there would exist a general accord on the questions on which agreement could be reached at the meeting and on practical steps leading to a fuller implementation of the Final Act. Proper preparations for the Madrid meeting and progress in reaching agreement on its decisions could serve as a basis for the participation of foreign ministers in their adoption. The socialist states believe that there are possibilities to conclude the Madrid meeting with mapping up practical steps relating to the military and political aspects of European security and to developing cooperation among all countries.

For a whole year now the governments of the participating countries of the European Conference have had before them the proposal to convene a conference on military détente and disarmament in Europe. The socialist countries have called on all the European Conference participants to take a constructive stand on the question of this conference so that it would be possible to adopt a decision on its convocation at the Madrid meeting. Naturally, they are prepared to study attentively proposals by other states on the procedure and content of work of that conference.

Being true to the Leninist policy of peaceful coexistence, friendship, and cooperation among peoples, the Soviet Union and the other socialist countries oppose the course of imperialist circles toward confrontation and military rivalry with their policy of easing tensions and normalizing and improving international relations. In the Warsaw Declaration they called on the participants in the European Conference to strictly observe all the provisions of the Final Act, and first of all the principles that they undertook to observe in mutual relations. The socialist countries thereby demonstrate their firm adherence to the accords that were agreed upon in Helsinki and their loyalty to the commitments assumed under the Final Act. We counter the "doctrine" of war hysteria and frenzied arms race with the doctrine of consistent struggle for peace and security on earth. We are true to the Peace Program set forth by the Twenty-fourth and Twenty-fifth Congresses of our Party. . . .

Vigorously working for strengthening peace and détente, the Soviet Union recently reaffirmed its interest in halting the dangerous turnabout, which appears imminent, following

NATO's decision to produce and deploy new American missiles in Western Europe. Confirming its earlier stated position on the most correct ways of resolving the issue of medium-range weapons in Europe, the Soviet Union, guided by the broad interests of peace and security, has proposed to start discussing the question of medium-range nuclear weapons simultaneously and in close connection with that of American forward-based nuclear weapons. This presupposes that possible accords reached on these issues can be practically implemented only following the entry into force of the SALT-II treaty.

The foreign policy of the socialist community, the USSR's consistent course for averting the danger of war, stopping the arms race, and developing friendly cooperation between states enjoy the full approval of the Soviet working people. This is evidenced by letters sent to the CPSU Central Committee. G. Krivulin, a Second World War veteran from Odessa, writes:

> I am not a Party member, but I fully support and approve of the foreign policy course of our Party and the other fraternal parties in the socialist countries aimed at preserving lasting peace on earth. Everything that is being done by the fraternal socialist countries and their parties for the sake of this humane aim serves the good of all the peoples of the world. This is well understood and highly appreciated by all peace-loving people on earth. As to the threats and intimidation by the imperialists, there is no point in trying to scare us: the strength and might of our state and of the socialist community have never been greater. And we are strengthening this might and will continue to strengthen it day after day.

Y. Kondratyuk, a foreman at a woodworking plant in Moscow, said in his letter to the CPSU Central Committee:

> My workmates and I unanimously approve and ardently support the peace-loving foreign policy of the Communist Party and the Soviet state. Like all the Soviet people we protest the militaristic course of the U.S. administration. The whole world sees that it is the Carter Administration that is deliberately trying to poison the international atmosphere with militarism, to spoil relations with our country. The enemies of peace are trying to sour relations between the Soviet Union and countries of Western Europe. But it is impossible to halt the process of détente.

The Soviet public sees its most important task in giving every support to the course for preserving and strengthening détente, for expanding peaceful cooperation between the peoples of Europe in accordance with the Final Act of the European Conference in Helsinki. . . .

In the present situation the CPSU Central Committee and the Soviet state are displaying a truly Leninist restraint, firmness, and principled position in upholding and pursuing the policy of preserving peace, ensuring the security of the Soviet people, and international security as a whole, while not falling for provocations, and yet repulsing imperialist claims.

The resolution of the June 1980 Plenary Session of the CPSU Central Committee, On the International Situation and the Foreign Policy of the USSR, expresses the conviction that there exist objective possibilities and sociopolitical forces capable of preventing the slide to a new cold war, of ensuring normal, peaceful coexistence between states with different social systems, and averting the threat of a world nuclear conflict. The road to the fulfillment of this task is the road of talks based on strict observance of the principle of equality and equal security. This fully applies to Soviet-American relations as well.

The peoples of the Soviet Union and the other socialist countries can work calmly and confidently in the knowledge that they have everything that is necessary for defending their gains, for repulsing the intrigues of imperialists. They can rest assured that the latest anti-Soviet campaign by the U.S. ruling circles and their attempts to divert the attention of the peoples from the threats to peace created by their own policy and military preparations will fail. Sooner or later the provocative actions will strike back at their instigators like a boomerang. In the conditions of the increasing threat to peace and freedom of the peoples and the unprecedented intensification of military activities by the United States and NATO in the world grows the realization of the need to pool the efforts of all progressive forces, of all peace champions against imperialism's dangerous plans.

The June 1980 Plenary Session of the CPSU Central Committee pointed out that in the present international situation the working class, the collective-farm peasantry, the intelligentsia, all the nations and nationalities of the Soviet Union rally closer around the Communist Party and ardently support the home and foreign policy of the CPSU and the Soviet state.

The peoples of the Soviet Union and the other socialist states look into the future with optimism. Inspired by the ideas of Marxism-Leninism they are preparing to meet the Twenty-sixth Congress of the Communist Party of the Soviet Union with new labor accomplishments. The Party Congress heralds a fresh upsurge of the Soviet economy and new steps to strengthen the country's defensive might.

The CPSU is drafting major plans for developing power generating industry, improving engineering, stepping up agriculture, and expanding the transport network. At the same time, it is intended to increase substantially the foreign trade turnover of the country and its participation in international efforts to promote economic ties.

The steady development of the economy creates new possibilities for strengthening the socialist community and expanding the USSR's economic ties with Eastern and Western countries. Coordinated programs of action in the field of international cooperation would furnish new opportunities for the optimal utilization of resources, development of leading branches of the economy, and protection of the environment.

It goes without saying that the vast plans of peaceful development require a favorable international situation. The current situation calls for vigorous joint actions by all peace loving forces to frustrate the plans of the opponents of détente and resist the imperialist policy of diktat and coercion.

The course of socialist countries for consolidating peace and the security of nations has taken deep roots and is supported by the mighty progressive forces of our time. . . .

To the Congress of the Communist Party of Cuba

The Soviet Union and the People's Republic of Cuba share relations of friendship and all-round cooperation and opinions on all key political problems. This was reaffirmed during the visit of the Soviet Communist Party delegation headed by Konstantin U. Chernenko to participate at the Second Congress of the Communist Party of Cuba. The following is an excerpt from a speech Konstantin Chernenko delivered on December 18, 1980 to the Second Congress of the Communist Party of Cuba.

The Soviet Union and the Republic of Cuba always share a feeling of comradeship in dealing with international affairs. . . . We have a common approach to all key problems of world politics.

We are making a consistent and determined effort to secure a lasting peace on earth and respect for the rights of all nations to free and independent development. The way to this lies in the policy of détente and peaceful cooperation of all states, in the implementation of practical disarmament measures, in the elimination of the hotbeds of conflicts, and in the settlement of disputed issues at the negotiating table.

The cause of international security has quite a few adversaries. These are, above all, the forces of imperialism and they have accomplices—dictatorial regimes, military juntas, and Peking's hegemony-seekers.

It is no simple task to consolidate peace. It requires much energy and perseverance to make the world political climate healthier. The socialist countries are ready to cooperate with broad political and social forces, with all countries which stand for normal good-neighborly relations. Of course, the basis of such cooperation can only be equality and equal security.

This was once again confirmed at the recent meeting of party and state leaders of the Warsaw Treaty member countries in Moscow.

The Soviet Union fully understands the just demands of the nonaligned movement which were so forcefully put forward in Havana where the sixth conference of this movement was held. Our support for the nonaligned movement as a positive factor of world politics was authoritatively confirmed during Leonid Brezhnev's recent visit to India.

Comrades, we are living in a rapidly changing world. No previous epoch has known such large-scale and dynamic changes. Before our very eyes social changes are, so to speak, knocking on the doors of the most tyrannical regimes. This is convincingly shown here, in Latin America, by the downfall of the dictatorships in Nicaragua and Grenada, the people's actions in El Salvador, and the growing will for independence and freedom on the part of all the nations of the continent.

The United States would like to oppose these changes with the "rapid deployment force" and with constant pressure on countries pursuing policies which are not to its liking. This is a dangerous course. And there is no more important task today than to counter it with the united might of all the peace-loving forces.

All of us realize that the world today is a restless one. The capitalist ideological centers try to make it appear as if the complications in international life are due to interference by the Soviet Union, Cuba, and other socialist countries in the internal affairs of other nations, to something like "export of revolution" on their part. This, of course, is utterly untrue.

Indeed, do the Cuban teachers who teach children in Nicaragua to read and write seek concessions for Cuba or lay their hands on the riches of that country? Have Cuba's brave sons rendered military assistance to independent Ethiopia and Angola, at the request of their governments, for the sake of depriving them of freedom or interfering in their internal affairs? No, a thousand times, no!

This is a truly internationalist policy; this is a policy of peace and comradely solidarity.

Neither you, nor we, nor other countries of socialism are engaged in the export of revolution. Revolutions are born and triumph on the soil of each particular country because of its internal conditions; they are not brought into a country from outside. But the export of counterrevolution and interference in the affairs of the socialist countries from outside are equally inadmissible. Imperialists should know this!

We communists believe in the power of reason and good will. Peace answers the innermost hopes of the whole of mankind, and the future can and must belong only to the policy of peace.

A convincing proof of this is the Soviet initiative on the normalization of the situation in the Persian Gulf zone. Agreement between the interested states on the basis of the concrete and constructive proposal put forward a few days ago by Leonid Brezhnev in his speech to the parliamentarians of India could eliminate the dangerous tension in one of the most explosive regions of the planet. . . .

At the Soviet-Cuban Friendship Meeting

During his visit to the People's Republic of Cuba, Konstantin U. Chernenko was invited to participate in the meeting of Soviet-Cuban Friendship at the José Martí Metalworks. Such meetings play an important role in familiarizing visiting delegations with the realities of life in the host country.

Following is an excerpt from the speech Konstantin Chernenko made at the meeting on December 19, 1980.

. . . The policy of the Communist Parties is a policy deeply reflecting the aspirations of the people. This fully applies to the Communists' international activities.

You know how many constructive ideas and proposals have been put forward by the Soviet Union, Cuba, and other countries of the socialist community in order to ensure a peaceful future for mankind. It was the fraternal socialist countries that initiated and promoted the policy of détente. In this policy lies the real possibility of improving the political climate in the world.

But the old world clings to old ways. Of late we have witnessed dangerous attempts by imperialist and reactionary forces to derail détente, whip up the arms race, and place obstacles in the way of progressive social changes.

Leonid Brezhnev, during his recent visit to India, said:

The question now is how will things develop further? If this negative and, let us say frankly, dangerous course continues, the world will be under a grave threat. But if reason will triumph, then a constructive policy which corresponds to the hopes of nations and the interests of all countries will again assert itself.

While being aware of the danger posed by imperialist policies, we are far from being pessimistic. Our confidence that the future belongs to peaceful relations between peoples and states rests on a firm foundation. Behind all the vicissitudes of events and sharp changes in the political barometer one cannot help seeing that the world is nevertheless becoming better.

This past year has been a difficult one for the policy of détente. And still, despite a certain cooling in the international climate, the trend of détente continues. Moreover, people in many countries are becoming more aware that it is important to preserve the fruits of détente and multiply them.

Is it not a fact that colonial empires have collapsed and the overwhelming majority of the countries in Asia, Africa, and Latin America have gained independence? It is a fact that the communist and working-class movement in capitalist countries is growing and getting stronger. And, of course, it is an important fact that the socialist community—a large and powerful family of free peoples—is developing and gaining strength.

The recent meeting of the leaders of the Warsaw Treaty member states in Moscow was a new vivid expression of the striving of the fraternal countries for peace and détente, and of their unity. The participants in the meeting expressed their firm determination not to permit a reversal of the course of development of international relations. This meeting shows that the fraternal socialist countries are vigilant. They will not allow anyone to undermine the peoples' socialist gains. The results of the Moscow meeting represent a new call for peace and a serious warning to those who provoke international conflicts.

The road to peace is a wide road where there is enough room for every country and every nation.

And we stand for pooling the efforts of all peace-loving states for the sake of ensuring a tranquil and peaceful future of our planet.

Cuba's vigorous foreign policy activities meet with full understanding in the Soviet Union. The great prestige of Cuba in the socialist community, in the nonaligned movement, and throughout the world results directly from the fact that Cuba is waging a consistent fight against arbitrariness in international relations and against neocolonialism and racism, and is pursuing a noble internationalist policy.

The Soviet Union stands for making the 1980s, and all subsequent years, a time of peace. We shall strive toward this goal together with Cuba, with all the fraternal socialist countries, with all the peace-loving forces of today. . . .

The Soviet Peace Program
for the 1980s

Every year on April 22nd the anniversary of Vladimir Lenin's birth is celebrated with large public meetings held in many cities and remote towns all over the Soviet Union. The major event broadcast by national TV is the grand meeting in the Moscow Palace of Congresses in the Kremlin. Communist Party leaders and members of the government deliver their speeches on the occasion, and then a gala concert takes place.

Following is an excerpt from the report made by Konstantin U. Chernenko at the commemorative meeting in Moscow, on April 22, 1981, dedicated to the 111th anniversary of Lenin's birth.

. . . In 1918, when the young Soviet Republic was less than a year old, Lenin wrote with lawful pride: "We as a socialist republic, even though ravaged and robbed by the imperialists, have remained outside the imperialist war and have raised aloft the banner of peace, the banner of socialism for all the world to see." Whatever challenges they have had to face, whatever trials they have had to withstand, the Soviet communists have always held this banner high. The Twenty-sixth CPSU Congress has demonstrated again that in foreign policy the Leninist Party confidently continues to pursue the Leninist line.

As is known, the beginning of the 1980s was marked by a serious aggravation of the international situation. The policy of imperialism, primarily of U.S. imperialism, threatens to reverse much of the progress made in the 1970s along the path of détente. Whipping up the arms race, the warlike circles of NATO are seeking to upset the prevailing military strategic balance between socialism and capitalism and to change in their favor the alignment of forces in the world. As a result, serious obstacles have been erected in the path of détente. The danger of war, which somewhat diminished in the middle of the last decade, has grown again.

Small wonder, therefore, that the Twenty-sixth Party Congress was awaited with tense attention. Would we over-react to provocation? What would Moscow say, how would it respond to Washington's provocative declarations and actions? This was a matter for guesswork and debates abroad on the eve of the Congress. Now the matter has been cleared up. The Twenty-sixth CPSU Congress has come forward with a comprehensive and constructive program for strengthening international security.

Preserving détente, curbing the arms race, and consoli-dating peace would meet the interests of all nations. Any nuclear conflict would cause untold suffering to mankind. This must not be allowed to happen. This is the essence of the approach of the CPSU to the most burning issue of today—the issue of war and peace.

Never before have weapons of such monstrous destruc-tive power been built up so rapidly as today. Never before have attempts to use them to settle disputes or conflicts threatened all civilization and even life on earth with extinc-tion.

From this one can make the following conclusion: to regard thermonuclear war as a rational and well-nigh "legal" extension of foreign policy is a crime. Today any responsible statesman is obliged to realize that reliance on brute force, on the use of nuclear weapons, puts mankind's existence in jeopardy.

Unfortunately, the statements and actions of some poli-ticians on both sides of the Atlantic show they either fail or refuse to understand this fact. Furthermore, by talking of a "limited," "closed" nuclear war they are seeking to bring people round to the idea that a nuclear missile conflict is a tolerable, acceptable option. This is why it is so important for the truth about the disastrous consequences of thermo-nuclear war to be fully realized by all nations. In view of this, the Twenty-sixth Party Congress approved the proposal to set up a prestigious international committee of leading sci-entists from various countries, who would show the absolute necessity of preventing nuclear war.

Reviewing the foreign policy program of the twenty-sixth Congress in general, one cannot fail to see that the line pursued by the CPSU in international affairs is not motivated by considerations of opportunity, nor is it subordinated to any narrow selfish objectives or directed against any people or state. It is a policy of opposition to war, to the forces of militarism and neocolonialism. Its objective is to safeguard peace and to normalize the world situation.

Now this program is being broadly discussed by parliaments, governments, parties, and the world public. I would like to touch upon a few issues in this context.

First, on a moratorium on the deployment of new medium-range nuclear missiles in Europe: there has been a plethora of words about this proposal in the West. It would seem, however, that this matter is as clear as daylight. If one is willing to negotiate an arms reduction sincerely and with hope of success, would it not be reasonable to freeze, if only for the period of the talks, armaments at their existing levels?

The problem of reducing nuclear missile forces in Europe was clearly outlined in Leonid Brezhnev's recent statement in Prague. The Soviet stance is essentially as follows: without upsetting the approximate military parity in the European continent, to try and scale it down gradually. . . .

There is another essential problem I wish to touch upon. In the United States they are stubbornly insisting that negotiations on specific issues should be conducted in the context of the full spectrum of international problems. Only recently the last U.S. administration expatiated on every issue without exception in the context of its thoroughly hypocritical concern for "human rights." Now we are being faced with new "contexts." What are the motives behind them, one may wonder? They are simple: to evade, for example, strategic arms limitation talks; to add fuel to conflicts; to interfere directly or indirectly in the internal affairs of other nations. Isn't the policy of the Reagan administration in relation to El Salvador or the undeclared war against the independent nonaligned Democratic Republic of Afghanistan sufficient evidence to this effect?

Or just take the machinations against socialist Poland. Some politicians in the West, on the one hand, connect the prospects for détente with the trend of developments in Poland and, on the other hand, are going out of their way to destabilize the situation in Poland and hamper that country's efforts to

Konstantin Chernenko in his study.

On February 14, 1984, heads of the foreign delegations who had arrived in Moscow for the funeral of Yuri Andropov, met Soviet leaders in the Kremlin. The photograph shows U.S. Vice-President George Bush, expressing his condolences to Konstantin Chernenko, General Secretary of the CPSU Central Committee.

Konstantin Chernenko with George Marchais, Secretary-General of the French Communist Party, at the mass rally of international solidarity held in Villejuif, a working-class suburb of Paris, February 5, 1982.

Konstantin Chernenko with Margaret Thatcher, Andrei Gromyko, and Geoffrey Howe (Secretary of State for Foreign and Commonwealth Affairs), February 14, 1984.

At a meeting between Konstantin Chernenko and Didier Ratsiraka, Secretary-General of the Vanguard of the Malagasy Revolution party, President of the Democratic Republic of Madagascar, on February 17, 1984, in Moscow.

Konstantin Chernenko with Fidel Castro, Andrei Gromyko, Konstantin Rusakov (secretary of the CPSU Central Committee), and Carlos Rafael Rodriguez (Vice-President of the Council of State and the Council of Ministers of the Republic of Cuba), February 15, 1984.

Konstantin Chernenko, who headed the CPSU delegation to the Twenty-fourth Congress of the French Communist Party, talks to Anatoli Karpov, world chess champion (third from right), when visiting Louvre, February 1982.

Konstantin Chernenko near Moscow, 1982.

Konstantin Chernenko with his wife, Anna Dmitriyevna, daughter, Yelena Konstantinovna, and grandson, Mitya, in the Crimea, 1982.

overcome the critical period. This is a hypocritical and adventurist stand. The Polish communists and the Polish working people have built a strong and independent socialist state; they will not surrender their gains. One would do well to remember that people's Poland has loyal friends it can rely upon.

Striving for a radical improvement of the international climate and coming forward with specific initiatives, the Soviet Union is not presenting anybody with ultimatums. It is by no means clinging to the "all or nothing" principle in this field. Soviet proposals are an invitation to negotiations, to a dialogue, in the course of which any initiatives can and must be discussed as long as they help find a solution to vital international problems. The Soviet Union is prepared for such a dialogue at all levels within the framework of its bilateral relations with the United States, France, the FRG, and other countries, as well as within the framework of the UN Security Council. As Leonid Brezhnev has recently emphasized, in so doing we are not imposing any preliminary conditions.

As for the attempts of certain Western circles to talk to us in a language of threats and their dangerous balancing between détente and the cold war, our Party declares firmly: we will not allow anybody to infringe on the legitimate interests of this country and our allies.

While working persistently to improve international relations the Soviet Union is not relaxing its vigilance. The twenty-sixth Congress put itself on record quite definitely to this effect. A strong shield is necessary to safeguard the peaceful life of the Soviet people and their allies. And we have such a shield: it is the valiant Soviet armed forces and the allied armies of the Warsaw Treaty member countries.

The Soviet Peace Program is planned for many years ahead. It is, in fact, already yielding very good results. It is inducing many governments again and again to reevaluate their positions on vital international issues. It is stimulating the activities of broad democratic and antiwar forces of different political affiliations. It gives people confidence that there is a realistic way out of the present tense situation.

Comrades, Lenin saw in the fusion of the struggle for peace with the struggle of peoples for social progress a realistic way of putting up a strong barrier against the imperialist policy of war, plunder, and violence. This approach provides our Party with a dependable guideline in international affairs today.

Our Party links its policy of peace with support for the rightful causes of freedom, democracy, and national independence. But nobody will ever be able to prove that the Soviet Union's assistance to other nations pursues any selfish ends. Such facts are nonexistent. Different facts are in evidence. Soviet specialists are spreading knowledge among people whom colonialism doomed to cultural degradation. Where poverty reigned supreme, industrial and agrarian centers are being born with Soviet assistance. Our support helps the peoples exposed to the coercive pressure of imperialism safeguard their independence. We can be justly proud of this internationalist, Leninist policy. And we do take pride in it.

In an interview with the American journalist Louise Bryant, Lenin said, "America will gain nothing from the pious Wilsonian policy of refusal to do business with us for the simple reason that our government is not to their liking." This statement has stood the test of time.

To plan a policy divorced from reality is a fruitless pursuit. Fantastic allegations about the Soviet Union's ambitions for "world supremacy" and "a world communist government" can only lead the cause of international communication and cooperation into a dangerous impasse. The hue and cry about "international terrorism" being masterminded by the Soviet Union is just as absurd. Those who are raising it are in fact setting up a smoke screen to conceal their scheme to launch an offensive against the national liberation movement.

The Soviet Union is coming out with determination for the universal recognition of international law standards. This is why we are opposed to those who may arrogate to themselves the right to teach a lesson to other nations, the right to suppress aspirations to freedom, be it in Asia, Africa, Latin America, or, indeed, any other part of the world. We reject "a code of conduct" which would throw mankind back to the long past epoch when international relations were subject to unchallenged domination by the imperialists, to blackmail and discrimination against weaker nations by stronger powers. Social progress can neither be stopped nor reversed.

In advancing the Peace Program for the 1980s the CPSU is fully determined to consolidate further the fraternal alliance of socialist nations. Our Party will continue its efforts to strengthen the international unity of the world communist movement, to expand and deepen its bonds of comradely cooperation with all Marxist-Leninist parties. Joint actions in the struggle against the arms race, for peace and social progress help ensure a peaceful future for mankind. The Soviet Union has always been and will be a loyal friend of all nations which are following their own path toward a life of justice in the struggle against imperialism and the forces of reaction.

It is difficult to establish a lasting peace without concerted efforts. Only a truly worldwide coalition of antiwar forces can cope with this task. Such a coalition is not a utopia. It is called into existence by the vital need for nations to join forces in the service of peace and to remove the danger of thermonuclear war. This country is prepared for broad and constructive cooperation with countries belonging to a different social system, with all those who are willing to work in good faith for a durable, just, and democratic peace.

Comrades, 20 years ago man for the first time overcame the forces of terrestrial gravitation. A human being saw this planet from outer space for the first time. It was Yuri Gagarin, our countryman, the pride of all mankind. The advent of the space age has not only opened up new vistas of knowledge. One has become much more keenly aware of the fact that the earth is the common home of human beings and must be taken care of by all of them together. The homeland of Lenin and Gagarin is seeking to ensure that the boundless potential of the human mind should be wholly devoted to this noble cause.

By the authority of the Twenty-sixth Congress the Communist Party of the Soviet Union has confirmed that the Soviet people's will towards peace, their allegiance to the ideals of freedom, are unshakable.

Leninism in Action

Soon after the Twenty-sixth Congress of the Communist Party of the Soviet Union, Konstantin U. Chernenko published his analysis of the comprehensive and constructive proposals for preserving peace, developing the process of détente, and curbing the arms race put forward by the Congress. The analysis appeared in the monthly journal Political Self-Education, *founded in 1957 in Moscow for presenting the texts of international documents, reports and commentaries, articles on the methodology of political studies, statistics for lecturers, etc. The monthly is immensely popular among students of political science. Its circulation is over 2 million copies.*

The following is an excerpt from the article by Konstantin Chernenko published in Political Self-Education *(no. 5, May 1981).*

The international policy of the CPSU ensures the necessary external conditions for carrying out the creative tasks confronting the Soviet people. The speech given by Leonid Brezhnev, and other documents of the Twenty-sixth Party Congress, are an elaboration of the consistently class-based, internationalist, and peace-loving Leninist policy of the CPSU in international relations. They contain a thorough and detailed analysis of the vital issues of world development and advance a concise and realistic program for averting the threat of war and consolidating peace and the security of the nations.

The beginning of the 1980s has been marked, as is well known, by a serious aggravation of the international situation.

The policy of imperialism, first and foremost U.S. imperialism, and of NATO's militant circles, threatens to wipe out much that was achieved for détente in the 1970s. By whipping up the arms race they intend to upset the existing military-strategic balance between socialism and capitalism and change the balance of power to their own advantage.

It is understandable why people throughout the world waited so anxiously to see what position the Twenty-sixth Congress of our Party would take in this worrying situation. And the Twenty-sixth Congress has come forward with comprehensive and constructive proposals for preserving peace, deepening détente, and restraining the arms race. The essence of the CPSU's approach to the most burning question of today—the question of war and peace—is clear: a worldwide nuclear conflict would bring humanity inestimable losses. All peace-loving forces must act together to prevent a military catastrophe.

Any responsible politician today must realize that to set one's hopes on the use of force, on the use of nuclear missile weapons, puts into question the future of the human race on earth. But unfortunately the attitudes and behavior of certain politicians on both sides of the Atlantic make it clear that they do not understand this or do not want to. That is why it is so important that the truth about the disastrous consequences of a thermonuclear conflict be fully realized by all the peoples. The Twenty-sixth CPSU Congress has proposed the setting up of an authoritative international committee of the most eminent scientists from various countries, which would show the absolute necessity of averting a thermonuclear catastrophe. Soviet scientists and Soviet public opinion are called upon to make a fitting contribution to this urgent matter.

Appraising the foreign policy program adopted by the Twenty-sixth CPSU Congress as a whole, one cannot help but see that the Party pursues a consistent and principled line in international affairs. It is not affected by considerations of the moment, not subject to any aims of narrow self-interest, nor directed against any people or state. Its main aim is the preservation of peace on earth. That is why the progressive public at large and all realistically minded politicians are calling for a careful study of the proposals put forward by the Congress and for giving a constructive answer to them.

The Soviet proposal for a moratorium on the deployment of medium-range missiles in Europe has attracted a great deal of attention among Western political circles and been given much space by newspapers and magazines in many countries. It could take effect before a permanent agreement on the limitation and—better still—reduction of nuclear weapons on both sides was concluded. The meaning of our proposal would seem perfectly clear: if you want to conduct negotiations on arms reduction, if you want to do it sincerely and with hope for success, then would it not be better, having commenced negotiations, to freeze the existing levels of armaments, if only for the period of negotiations? After all, it is quite obvious that to conduct negotiations on arms reduction is far more difficult when new missiles in their tens and hundreds are about to be aimed at you. Some people, furthermore, put forward the idea that the Soviet Union has forged ahead in medium-range nuclear missiles and, allegedly, that is why it aspires to preserve the balance of power at the present level. The absurd assertion is being spread that the Soviet Union is withdrawing its proposals made in Berlin in the autumn of 1979. . . .

The essence of the Soviet position is, without upsetting the approximate military balance that has taken shape on the European continent, to achieve a lowering of its level step by step. One cannot help emphasizing, however, that the West has not yet given a constructive answer to the Soviet initiatives. On whom then does the blame for the arms race lie?

Having proposed at the Twenty-sixth Congress that the area to be covered by confidence building measures be extended to the Urals, the Soviet Union has gone a long way towards meeting the wishes of the Western powers. In this way we hope to improve the political climate in Europe and facilitate the convening of a European conference on disarmament. The Soviet Union has a right to expect that the Western powers meet trust with trust and advance their own proposals on extending the area for confidence building measures further to the West, which will match our step. The Soviet Union is ready, as before, to negotiate on extending confidence building measures also to the Far East. The problem of improving the situation in this vast and troubled region remains urgent, and it is necessary, indeed essential, to continue looking for a way to solve it.

Of the utmost urgency is the following, very important question: in the West, first and foremost in the United States, they persist in their view that negotiations on specific vital issues should be "linked" with the whole spectrum of international problems. Only recently, the previous American administration linked absolutely everything with a totally spurious campaign for the "defense of human rights." Now new "linkages" are in circulation, evidently designed to justify evasion of negotiations on strategic arms limitation, the stirring up of conflict situations, and direct or indirect interference in the internal affairs of other countries. In our view, this is borne out by the Reagan administration's policy toward El Salvador and its provocations against independent, nonaligned Afghanistan.

The fuss surrounding socialist Poland is not conducive towards an improvement in the international situation either. Certain officials in the West, on the one hand, make the prospects for détente hang on the events in Poland, and on the other, they try to destabilize the situation there and make it hard for the country to overcome the crisis period. This is a hypocritical and provocative policy. The Polish communists and working people have built a strong, independent socialist homeland and one can be sure that they will be able to defend their historical achievements. And in this, as the twenty-sixth Congress has stressed, our Polish friends can firmly count on the support of their allies.

Acting with all due persistence in the interests of improving the international climate, the Soviet Union is not relaxing its vigilance. Our Party's attitude to the attempts of particular Western circles to talk to us in the language of force, to their dangerous balancing between détente and the cold war, was expressed fully and clearly at the twenty-sixth Congress: we will not allow anyone to infringe upon the legitimate interests of our country and its allies. To guarantee a peaceful life for the Soviet people and their allies a strong shield is necessary, and we have one—it is the valiant Soviet Armed Forces and the allied armies of the member countries of the Warsaw Treaty.

The Soviet Peace Program for the 1980s is only just beginning to be realized, but one very important thing has already been done. The Program has instilled confidence in people that there is a realistic way out of the tense situation that has arisen in the world today. It has served as a powerful stimulus for rousing the broad, democratic, antiwar forces of various political persuasions. It has demonstrated once again that our country and its socialist allies are the main bulwark of peace on earth.

The participants in the forum of Soviet communists, and all who followed its work with undivided attention, must definitely remember the concrete serious discussion about the development of the world socialist system, about the cares and concerns with which fraternal countries are preoccupied today. The interest in this is natural: the Soviet Union together with the countries of the socialist community are building a new world made up of historically unprecedented types of genuinely just, equal, and fraternal relations between peoples and states.

With the development of cooperation much that is new has become part of life in the socialist countries, part of the life of literally every individual citizen, making it more colorful, interesting, and varied. Now practice is putting new tasks before the socialist countries. And first and foremost, note should be taken of the extremely important step which the socialist countries are about to take: to supplement coordination of plans with coordination of the economic policy as a whole.

The life-giving force of friendship and cooperation based on Marxism-Leninism and proletarian internationalism, and on mutual trust strengthened in shared experiences, is a significant factor at the present stage of socialist construction. At the Twenty-sixth Congress of the CPSU it was stressed with all due force and urgency that it is important to study carefully and make wide use of the interesting and valuable experience accumulated in the socialist countries. Learning from one another is the order of the day, a huge reserve which should be used fully when tackling major and complex questions which have been raised on today's agenda: the intensification of the economy; the implementation of important social programs; and the development of the working people's communist consciousness.

Experience teaches us that for the progressive development of socialist society it is essential to enhance the leading role of the Party, to hark to the voice of the masses, to fight decisively against all manifestations of bureaucratism and voluntarism, actively to develop socialist democracy, to conduct a considered and realistic policy in foreign economic relations, and to strengthen in every way the fraternal unity of the countries of socialism. This is all the more important, since the West is now employing a whole set of measures calculated to undermine and erode the socialist system.

Lenin always emphasized the necessity of organically combining the policy of peace with support for the just cause of freedom, democracy, and national independence. In the merging of the struggle for peace with the struggle of the peoples for social progress, Lenin saw a real possibility of firmly blocking the imperialist policy of war, plunder, and coercion. This approach serves as a reliable guide for the CPSU's international policy.

The CPSU Central Committee's Report to the twenty-sixth Congress outlined a wide area of cooperation between the Soviet Union and countries freed from colonial oppression, the countries of socialist orientation, those that have chosen the path of socialist development. The most important milestones on this path are the gradual liquidation of the positions of the imperialist monopolies in these countries, of the powerful bourgeoisie and feudal lords, the winning by the people's state of commanding heights in the economy and the transition to a planned development of productive forces, and encouragement of the cooperative movement in the villages. The basis for the progressive changes in public life are the enhanced role of the working masses and the gradual strengthening of the state apparatus by national cadres who are devoted to the people. The anti-imperialist nature of the foreign policy of these states is- close to the Soviet Union. The CPSU is increasing and extending its cooperation with their revolutionary parties.

The Soviet Union firmly advocates respect for generally accepted international norms. That is exactly why we do not recognize anyone's right to "teach lessons" to other nations, the right to suppress their will for freedom, whether in Asia, Africa, or Latin America—any corner of the globe. The objective course and outcome of the class struggle in one or another country may take and takes shape differently. But one thing is certain: there can be no turning back to that period when international relations were governed solely by imperialist dictation, blackmail, and the discrimination of the weak by the strong.

Of course, no one will succeed in reversing the course of time, but imperialism, by weakening the front of the anti-imperialist forces, is unquestionably attempting to slow it down, to damp the heat of anti-imperialist struggle. In recent years bourgeois propaganda has spared no effort to undermine the unity of the international Communist and working-class movement and to drive a wedge between the CPSU and the fraternal parties. Differences of opinion on some or other questions, which naturally can and do arise among communists in various countries, have been exaggerated in every possible way. The stream of inventions and slander, however, have struck a powerful obstacle—the power of truth. It rang out with a mighty voice at Twenty-sixth CPSU Congress, an event which became an exciting demonstration of proletarian internationalism and of the militant solidarity of communists from all continents.

The speeches given at the Party's twenty-sixth Congress by our guests representing the delegations of Communist and workers' parties showed that the successes scored by these parties are largely determined by their ability to use and apply the Leninist theoretical heritage and Leninist methodology in appraising the class and political forces in the specific political situation in their countries. The power of the blows which the revolutionary forces are dealing imperialism in its strongholds depends of course on the ideological maturity, unity, and cohesion of these parties. A careful attention to theory, to Marxist-Leninist teaching, to its internationalist meaning, and to the successes achieved on this basis has always been and will continue to be an important factor of social progress in any country and on any continent. Without it no socialist revolution can be victorious.

As the influence of the Communist parties grows, so the tasks confronting them become more complex and diverse, and this gives rise to different appraisals and sometimes to discussions between parties. Practice will show who was right and who was mistaken. Differences of this nature between parties should not be dramatized, nor should they set them in opposition to one another. It goes without saying that if it is a matter of fundamental differences, no compromises are possible. Each Party chooses the path leading to socialism in conformity with the national and specific historical conditions of its country. But of course one must not forget the general laws of revolution and socialist construction. It is important to study carefully and objectively the experience of real socialism and not permit distortion of it. . . . The CPSU will extend and deepen the ties of comradely internationalist cooperation with all Marxist-Leninist parties. Concerted action with them in the struggle against the arms race, for peace and social progress, for our common class aims benefits the future of humanity.

Peace can and must be strengthened by acting together. Only a genuinely worldwide coalition of antimilitarist forces is capable of achieving this. Such a coalition is quite feasible. Life itself, and the need for the peoples to unite in the struggle for peace against the threat of thermonuclear war, demands it. In the present situation this is the most important prerequisite of social progress, of the triumph of our communist ideals. . . .

To the Voters of the Kuibyshev Constituency in Moscow

The following is an excerpt from a speech delivered by Konstantin U. Chernenko to the voters of the Kuibyshev constituency in Moscow on November 23, 1981 during the election campaign for the USSR Supreme Soviet.

As regards certain questions of the foreign policy activities of our Party, I would like to stress that the program of economic and social development of our country put forward by the Twenty-sixth Party Congress is being implemented in complicated international conditions. There is no more important task now than to preserve and consolidate peace, détente, and international security. This task is in the focus of attention of the CPSU Central Committee.

Consider the following fact: for 36 years now the peoples of the Soviet Union have lived in peace. It has not been easy to attain this. It has been necessary to find solutions to the most stubborn conflicts and search for ways of eliminating the cold war, mistrust, and enmity in international relations. Profound optimism and a creative approach were needed to work out and substantiate the Peace Program and make it an effective instrument of détente. Abroad the Peace Program is often called "Brezhnev's plan of peace offensive." The great international authority of the leader of the CPSU and the Soviet state is reflected in this.

Man cannot live just for the day. He thinks about what tomorrow will be like and what awaits him in the future. Therefore the concern of many people today for the destiny of their countries and for the destiny of the present and future generations is quite understandable. Imperialism is directly to blame for the poisoning of the political climate in the world. The administration in the U.S. is especially responsible for this. It was this administration that dramatically whipped up the arms race in an attempt to change the military and political balance of international forces in its favor. It is this administration that seeks to bring about a dangerous confrontation between the U.S., on the one hand, and the Soviet Union, world socialism, and all of the forces of national and social liberation, on the other.

Let us take, for example, the European continent. Here, twice in this century, imperialists unleashed bloody world wars. These wars carried off tens of millions of lives. Today, too, the aggressive forces want to turn Europe into a dangerous powder keg. The proof of this is NATO's decision to deploy in Western Europe about 600 U.S. medium-range nuclear missiles in addition to the U.S. forward-based weapons already stationed there. It is clear that the United States seeks to trample down the principles of equality and equal security and to achieve military superiority over the Soviet Union.

It is obvious that such designs are futile. In replying to questions put by the editor of the West German magazine *Der Spiegel,* Leonid Brezhnev said that ''it would be better to give up dreams of attaining military superiority over the USSR.''

Our position with regard to mankind's most urgent problem, that of curbing the nuclear arms race and limiting nuclear arms, was clearly stated in this interview. The Soviet Union stands for the conscientious implementation of the second Treaty on the limitation of strategic offensive arms (SALT-II). We have put forward a proposal on banning all tests of nuclear weapons and their production, as well as the development and manufacture of any new types of weapons of mass destruction, including neutron weapons. As you know, comrades, concrete measures on easing tension and eliminating the seats of conflicts in Central Europe, the Far East, the Persian Gulf zone, and the Indian Ocean were set forth in Leonid Brezhnev's report at the twenty-sixth Congress and in other speeches. As a result of our Party's efforts, Soviet-U.S. talks on the limitation of nuclear arms in Europe will begin in late November. It is our hope that the SALT talks will follow.

Of course, these talks will not be easy. Reagan's latest speech, in which he put forward the so-called initiative on medium-range missiles, is a clear indication of this. Frankly, such a speech is evidently intended for simpletons and is nothing but a piece of propaganda. Naturally, this is no basis for talks and we have openly said so for all the world to hear.

The madness of nuclear militarism, and the military and political adventurism of the United States, is opposed by the Soviet state's firm and consistent approach to the solution of international problems. This is the way of honest and genuine talks on all disputed issues, of reaching mutually acceptable agreements, and of broad and equal cooperation in the interests of the peoples. As the practice of international relations convincingly shows, personal contacts between heads of state and government yield good results. Leonid Brezhnev's current official visit to the FRG will no doubt have a favorable influence on the political climate in Europe.

Of course, the development of Soviet-West German contacts is not to everyone's liking in the West. They are not to the liking especially of those who are ready to sacrifice to militarism the security and well-being of the people of the FRG and other West European countries and make them the United States's nuclear hostages.

The Reagan administration is trying in every way to evade answering the Soviet Union's direct and honest question: is it ready for constructive talks on curbing the arms race and is it ready to stop nuclear blackmail? A spate of propaganda is unleashed in reply. Some prominent U.S. legislators and scientists have described such an approach on the part of the Reagan administration as "militarist psychosis" fraught with danger for the United States itself. They rightly point out that increasing the U.S. military budget to an astronomical sum of hundreds of billions of dollars means taking money away from measures for solving America's acute economic and social problems and will in the near future result in a further exacerbation of the crisis of American society. But the U.S. leaders do not heed the voice of reason. They try to divert public attention from their plans for escalating the arms race and from the internal contradictions of capitalism by intensifying the so-called psychological warfare against the Soviet Union and other socialist countries.

Today one of the main targets of imperialist interference and pressure is Poland. The events in Poland are used by our class adversaries for instilling in people the false notion of the "untenability" of socialism. But it was not socialism, either as a doctrine or as a social system that exists in reality, that gave rise to the events in Poland. . . . The root of the trouble lies in a departure from the principles of socialist construction and violation of the Leninist standards of Party activity.

We are firmly convinced that the Polish United Workers' Party and the Polish working class will be able to overcome the considerable difficulties that have arisen. The working people of the Soviet Union and other countries of the socialist community are on their side.

The subversive activities of U.S. imperialism against another socialist country—the Republic of Cuba—have recently grown in intensity. I was in Cuba last year when I headed a CPSU delegation to the Second Congress of the Communist Party of Cuba. We visited industrial enterprises and educational institutions there, and met with workers, young people, and Cuban leaders. And everywhere we saw tremendous enthusiasm and the determination of the Cubans to work for peace and the strengthening of free socialist Cuba. We will long remember a meeting held in Havana, attended by 1 million people, to sum up the results of the Second Congress of the Communist Party of Cuba. It is difficult to describe its atmosphere in words. It had to be felt; one had to see the inspired faces and the sparkling eyes of the Cubans. In response to Comrade Fidel Castro's call, the participants in the meeting in a single outburst of fervor swore to defend the island of freedom to the last drop of their blood, to their last breath. It is impossible to overcome such people!

Today the propaganda services of the United States have again launched a vicious and slanderous anti-Cuban campaign. Washington threatens to tighten the economic blockade of the island of freedom. The open threats against Cuba are accompanied by provocative displays of the United States' naval power. It seems that the Reagan administration has decided to return to those methods of putting crude pressure on revolutionary Cuba which brought about the shameful defeat of U.S. policy toward that country back in the early 1960s. It seems that the present Washington administration is incapable of taking the lessons of the past into consideration and forgets that Cuba is an inalienable part of the socialist community.

The undeclared war waged by the forces of imperialism and hegemonism against the Democratic Republic of Afghanistan has been going on for several years now. This war was unleashed not only with the aim of depriving the Afghan people, who are friendly to us, of the gains of the April Revolution. This is not just the export of counterrevolution to a country that has cast off the fetters of dependence on imperialism. This is also an attempt to carry out the old plans of international reactionary forces of making Afghanistan a base for subversive activities and aggression against the Soviet Union. But these plans are doomed to failure. In rendering to its southern neighbor, at its request, all-round assistance, including military assistance, our country is fulfilling its internationalist duty to revolutionary Afghanistan and safeguards the security of its southern borders in the face of imperialist threat. Our Party's principled position in this regard rests on the full understanding and unanimous support of the Soviet people.

Soviet army units are in Afghanistan temporarily. They will be withdrawn subject to agreement with the Afghan leadership as soon as aggressive actions from outside stop and reliable guarantees are worked out, that they will not be resumed. A comprehensive political settlement is necessary. The peaceful initiatives of Afghanistan's government are a good basis for this.

Comrades, the world system of socialism has proved its vitality and its political dynamism. Not a single major international problem can be solved today without its participation. Herein lies our greatest gain and the objective nature of the processes of contemporary social and political development. World socialism cannot be intimidated. It has a sufficient economic and military potential to repel any threats. But our Party does not think that a nuclear war is inevitable. A broad front of antiwar and antimissile movement is growing in the world today. Representatives of different political parties and people of different views and religious beliefs are taking part in it. At times they have opposite political convictions. But they are united by an understanding of what nuclear weapons are and what a nuclear catastrophe is. Concerned about the future of human civilization, they show support for Leonid Brezhnev's call for talks and renunciation of confrontation, for banning nuclear weapons, and for halting the arms race.

The will of the peoples of the world and the Soviet people's unanimous approval of the foreign policy course of the CPSU strengthen confidence and the Communist Party's determination to continue firmly and persistently in its efforts to implement the Peace Program approved by the Twenty-sixth CPSU Congress.

At the International Solidarity Forum in Paris

On February 5, 1982, in a workers' suburb outside Paris, a mass meeting of international solidarity was held. The French Communists gathered at this meeting gave a warm welcome to the delegation of the Soviet Communist Party, headed by Konstantin U. Chernenko, which had been invited to the Twenty-fourth French Communist Party Congress

In his speech delivered at the meeting he tackled some problems concerning the social and economic development of the Soviet Union. Konstantin U. Chernenko reaffirmed that the peaceful policy line of the Communist Party of the Soviet Union and the Soviet Government is constant.

Imperialism has challenged us. The United States aims to destroy the established equilibrium, to achieve military superiority over the Soviet Union.

Despite what is said about us in the West, we, for our part, have never aimed and never will aim towards military superiority. We have not been and will not be the initiators of the arms race. The Soviet military threat, which they make so much fuss about in Washington, has never existed, does not exist, and never will!

But, of course, we have to strengthen our ability to defend ourselves, and, as you can understand, this demands special means and efforts.

We have to help our many friends. Take Poland for example. We consider that the true friends of the Polish people are called upon at this time to the task of helping them overcome their crisis. Only those who wish to hinder the normalization of the situation in Poland can create obstacles and even undermine economic relations with it through all kinds of "sanctions." I want to tell you that the Soviet Union has increased its political support and economic assistance to the Polish People's Republic to a significant degree. We consider it our international duty, and this is a duty we shall fulfill!

However, whatever conditions may arise, you can be absolutely certain, comrades, that our Party has not abandoned, and will not abandon, its principles, its main motto: "Everything for the Good of Man!"

There are many countries in the world today—I'm talking about the capitalist world—where social programs are being cut, where the workers' living standards are falling. And this is happening according to the wishes of their governments, but first and foremost, according to the wishes of military monopolies.

We in the Soviet Union are taking a completely different road. Our Party considers and considered that social programs must be implemented. And this is how it is done in our country.

Within a year after the Twenty-sixth Party Congress we adopted measures in accordance with which there has been an improvement in the material well-being of 4.5 million families with many children. Fourteen million pensioners have received pension increases. Within a year two million flats have been built. This means that 10 million people were able to move to new living quarters. Real per capita incomes have risen by 3.3 percent.

In social policy questions, as in all others, our Party has a complete unity of views with the people. This is not surprising—it is the policy which reflects the wishes and demands of the people, and this policy is being carried out by the working people of our country themselves. In the Communist Party's unity of thought and deed with the people we see the sense and reality of social democracy. In accordance with this, we are seeking to achieve ever growing participation of the part of the working people in managing all production, public, and state affairs. This aim is set forth in our Fundamental Law—the Constitution of the USSR.

As you know, a great deal is being said in the world now about victorious socialism. Of course it is spoken of in different ways. Time and again our opponents try to look for some crisis of socialism. Unfortunately, some people believe it. They maintain that socialism has reached a deadlock. And in America certain responsible officials even maintain that communism's days are already numbered.

We can assure you of this: they will have to be disappointed yet again! Socialism is advancing. It is being strengthened and is developing. At this very time it is accumulating new strength for further advancement, and this, of course, gives birth to new, bigger, by no means easy, but extremely interesting theoretical and practical problems. The CPSU is working on them, is looking for and finding the optimum solutions which guarantee the growth of socialism on a new level and on a new scale.

I understand, of course, that to argue seriously with those who are waiting impatiently for the end of communism is a waste of time. Life has shown how right we are, and we are deeply convinced that socialism—in those forms, of course, which correspond to the traditions and conditions of each country—will break more and more new ground. The future belongs to the society that serves the man of labor!

Comrades, I have already said a few words about the general international situation. Comrade Georges Marchais has spoken in detail about this subject in his report to the Congress.

Today's attempt by the most aggressive forces of imperialism to obstruct the path towards social progress by means of force and by means of military pressure carries with it the potential threat of a new world war. Today this threat looks more real, perhaps, than in the past. Why do we say this?

First and foremost, it is well known that the amount of weapons which has already been built up by imperialism and which exists on our planet has already exceeded all reasonable limits. Meanwhile, the West continues the arms race, which is not simply a matter of the further accumulation of weapons of mass destruction, but of these weapons becoming ever more dangerous and monstrous. The application of these new weapons can put into question everything which humanity has done in its conscious history.

Furthermore, plans for a nuclear war have long since been made in U.S. and NATO headquarters. But they have never before talked about them aloud so openly as before. Never before have U.S. generals and politicians talked so much and with such cynicism about the possibility of a limited nuclear war in Europe, about making a first or pre-emptive strike against socialism. This means that the process of militarization in the West has entered a new, far more dangerous phase.

We note that imperialism is not only getting ready for a major conflict on a worldwide scale, but at the same time is more extensively applying the big stick policy on a day-to-day basis. It is, first and foremost, a matter of attempting to suppress by armed force those fighting for national liberation.

Finally, a new element in the contemporary situation, which increases the danger of war, is the massive anti-Soviet, anticommunist campaign which has been whipped up not only by the mass media, but by the ruling circles in the United States and certain other NATO countries. The systematic and cunning kindling of hostility towards the Soviet Union and the other socialist countries is aimed at throwing humanity back to the atmosphere of the "cold war."

It must be said that this campaign, the policy of brinkmanship, is already having a baneful effect on the struggle for social progress and on social changes which take place in various countries.

The policy of imperialism must be rebuffed. It is essential to stop the destruction of the foundation of détente, and the undermining of peaceful relations between nations. It is essential to turn back again to détente, to stabilize peaceful coexistence.

We Soviet communists are directed to this very aim by the Peace Program for the 1980s as proclaimed by the Twenty-sixth Congress of the CPSU.

At an Awards Ceremony in the City of Tbilisi

The following is an excerpt from a speech delivered by Konstantin U. Chernenko on October 29, 1982 at a ceremony awarding the city of Tbilisi the Order of Lenin, the highest award in the Soviet Union. Tbilisi, located in the Caucasus, is the capital of the Georgian Soviet Socialist Republic, one of the 15 constituent republics of the Soviet Union.

. . . The general picture of what is now taking place in the international arena is extremely complex, dynamic, and contradictory. However, against the background of this motley picture and the tempestuous course of events one can easily discern two main, deep lying tendencies, the clash between which determines the political climate of today.

At one pole of world politics are all those who are for the prevention of a nuclear war, the cessation of the arms race, the solution of controversial issues through constructive negotiations; in other words, those who are for international détente and peaceful coexistence.

At the other pole are all those who would like to torpedo détente, whip up the arms race, and go back to the years of the cold war. There are not many of these politicians of yesterday, but they are dangerous. They are dangerous especially because the huge war machine, first of all in the United States, is in their hands.

The stake on the use of force, open support for tyrannic, repressive regimes, the course for the achievement of military superiority, a scornful attitude toward the interests of other states and peoples and insolent forcing upon them of its own imperial will—such is the policy of official America today.

Probably many people are puzzled: what has happened? It was not so long ago when U.S. presidents did not shun the word "détente." Let us recall the first half of the 1970s. At that time, over the course of several years, a solution had been found to some of the most complex problems both within the framework of Soviet-U.S. relations and within the framework of European politics. And immediately the world climate became more tranquil. People began to breathe more easily. This is what détente means. . . .

So what has happened? To be brief, I would answer this question in the following way: the American ruling class has failed to withstand the test of détente, the test of peaceful cooperation.

And indeed, détente is a many-sided, multifaceted process. It is unquestionably a road that leads to peace and cooperation. But not only this. The Soviet Union holds that détente opens the way to the democratization of international life in general and stimulates the political activity of the broad masses of the people. Détente is inseparable from a recognition of the right of every nation independently to decide its fate, to choose for itself the way of life and the direction of social development.

It is reactionary utopia, and nothing more, to hope to preserve, to "freeze" the social and political status quo. This has been convincingly proved by experience.

Here is a far from complete picture of the social changes which have taken place in the last ten years: the formation of a united socialist Vietnam; the liquidation of the dictatorial regimes in Portugal, Spain, and Greece; the collapse of the Portuguese colonial empire and the formation of independent Angola and Mozambique; the revolutions in Ethiopia, Afghanistan, and Iran; and the victory of the Sandinistas in Nicaragua.

All this has alarmed American reactionaries. The U.S. ruling circles considered each strike at tyranny as a strike at the political positions and the authority and influence of Washington. Certainly, there are many sober-minded people in the United States. They have warned against the danger of identifying U.S. interests with the interests of dictators and puppets. They have called for imperial ambitions to be abandoned, facts to be faced, and U.S. policies to be adapted to the new and changing world. However, these sensible voices have been drowned in the nationalistic and chauvinistic chorus. Not to adapt U.S. policies to the realities of the surrounding world, but to make this world adapt to the imperialist interests of the monopolies and subordinate it to them—that is how the new administration puts the matter.

For almost two years the U.S. rulers have "flexed their muscles." For almost two years Washington has poured abuse on the Soviet Union and other socialist countries. For almost two years the myths about the "Soviet threat" and "the hand of Moscow" have served as a kind of ideological foundation for U.S. foreign policy. What has Washington achieved by this? Probably it now has still more nuclear bombs. One military program outstrips another. But this does not make the U.S. international positions any stronger. On the contrary.

Let us look at some facts.

The cynical talk by American politicians about "limited," "protracted," and "rational" nuclear missile war and the intention to limit this war to the "European theater of war" have led to growing anxiety and uneasiness in Western Europe. They have also given rise to a wave of anti-American sentiments. The crude attempt of the White House to wreck the "gas pipes" contract poured additional oil on the flames. Certainly, the class and social foundations of trans-Atlantic solidarity have been preserved. But people on this side of the Atlantic ever more often ponder over the consequences of the excessive aggressiveness of the United States.

New areas of tension have appeared in relations between the United States and Latin America. Washington's support for the British colonial adventure in the South Atlantic puzzled even those who used to extol the policies of the "big North American brother." Central America is seething. Protest against the burdensome economic tribute which the peoples of the South American continent are forced to pay to the U.S. monopolies is growing.

The fraternizing of Washington with racist South Africa, and attempts to block the granting of independence to Namibia, have not at all enhanced the United States's prestige on the African continent.

What about the Middle East? Everybody understands that without the support and backing of Washington Israel would not have dared to resort to genocide against the people of Palestine and to drown long suffering Lebanon in blood. Today Americans are going through contortions: while defending and justifying the anti-Arab policies of Tel Aviv and coming out against the creation of an independent Palestinian state they simultaneously want to pass for friends of the Arabs.

The Arab world is, unfortunately, not united and is weakened by clashes of various interests and intentions. This is what the United States and Israel, now together and now separately, are playing on. In terms of strategy, however, the United States, which supports an unjust and unrightful cause, is fighting a losing battle.

More cracks have appeared in Japanese-United States relations. Incidentally, the number of such cracks in relations between Japan and several other countries has not diminished because of its turn toward militarization under the prompting of Washington. Such are the facts.

The authors of U.S. policy can easily add huge foreign policy deficit to the one hundred million [dollar] budget deficit, to the record number of unemployed, to the wave of bankruptcies, and other crisis phenomena. The matter went so far that one of the American newspapers came up with this comment. It said that if Moscow succeeded in putting its agents in the White House it would not be able to do more to undermine U.S. authority than is done by the present administration. That is where, it seems, one has to look for "the hand of Moscow."

The Soviet Union counters the bellicose, great power, and extremely egoistic foreign policy course of the United States with a confident, consistent, and time-tested policy, one free from time serving twists and turns. . . .

Our country's policy in Europe is based on the necessity to preserve the achievements of détente and to preserve and multiply all that has been gained and put down on paper in Helsinki. Successful completion of the Madrid meeting of participant-states in the European Conference would greatly help make the political situation in Europe healthier.

We are for a just and comprehensive settlement of the Middle East conflict, a settlement based on the guaranteed security of all the countries of the region, including an independent Palestinian state.

Our policy toward Third World countries rests on a realization of the inevitability and fruitfulness of progressive social changes. We actively support the struggle of the peoples for equitable and mutually advantageous cooperation, cooperation that is free from even the slightest traces of discrimination.

We are sincere in our desire to normalize relations with our great Chinese neighbor and are convinced that it will serve the interests both of China and the Soviet Union as well as the cause of world peace.

The Soviet Union is against the further escalation of tension in Soviet-U.S. relations. We are for normalizing and improving these relations. We are prepared to enter into businesslike and substantial negotiations with account taken of the interests of both sides. And we are confident that it would be possible to reach agreement on any question, provided our partners stop living in a world of illusions and entertaining hopes of achieving superiority and display a sense of responsibility and political wisdom.

If Washington is unable to rise above primitive anticommunism and continues to pursue a policy of threats and diktat, well, we are strong enough and we can wait. Neither sanctions nor military postures can frighten us. We believe in reason. And we believe that sooner or later, and the sooner the better, reason will triumph and the danger of war will be averted.

Sixty Years of Fraternal Friendship among Peoples

The following is an excerpt from an article by Konstantin U. Chernenko published in the Soviet monthly journal World Marxist Review *(no. 12, December 1982).*

All the peoples of the world are today faced with a common task whose significance to the destiny of humankind cannot be overestimated. This is the task of averting a world war, a thermonuclear holocaust. Lasting peace on earth is the central aim of Soviet foreign policy. Leonid Brezhnev's constructive proposals and initiatives in the last few months of his life on behalf of the Soviet Union are evidence of the inexhaustible energy the CPSU and the Soviet government are putting into the quest for ways and means of eliminating the danger of war, preserving and developing détente, bridling the arms race, and achieving an overall improvement of the system of international relations.

Soviet foreign policy has the understanding and support of large segments of the world's political forces and public opinion. This is a crucial factor enhancing the efficacy of our policy of peace. The CPSU attaches great significance to having international problems settled not only through government-to-government negotiations, through the efforts solely of diplomats. World politics, Lenin said time and again, must be the international affair of the masses. Accordingly, our party steadfastly advocates the international unity of all sociopolitical forces prepared and able to contribute to the consolidation of peace.

Harmonizing with the principal democratic interest of the peoples, that of preserving world peace, internationalism is entirely in accord with the class content of the CPSU's international strategy; i.e., proletarian internationalism and solidarity with fraternal socialist states and the revolutionary, anti-imperialist, liberation forces. . . .

Peace and cooperation among nations. Are these an ideal or a reality? If this question is approached from the standpoint of the general situation in the modern world, the reply prompts itself: they are still a dream, an ideal. But the 60-year history of the USSR and the international experience of socialism strikingly demonstrate that this ideal is attainable. To turn it into a global reality is no easy matter.

As for our country, the Soviet Union, it will continue to follow the course set by the Twenty-sixth Party Congress, the course of the Peace Program for the 1980s, as it was said at the Extraordinary Plenary Session of the Central Committee of the Communist Party of the Soviet Union, which met in connection with the untimely death of Leonid Brezhnev. Détente, disarmament, the overcoming of situations of conflict, and removal of the threat of nuclear war, those are the tasks we have set ourselves, it was said at the Plenary session. We want reliable security for ourselves, for our friends, for all the peoples of the world.

The CPSU, Society, Human Rights

The following is an excerpt from Konstantin U. Chernenko's book published in 1982 by one of the largest Soviet book publishers— Novosti Press Agency Publishing House. Approximately a thousand titles are published annually in 35 languages, with a total circulation of over 20 million copies.

. . . In recent years imperialism has put forward the idea of the "struggle for the defense of human rights" allegedly trampled underfoot in the socialist countries, particularly in the USSR.

The U.S.-organized campaign in "defense" of human rights, which allegedly are violated in the socialist countries, and especially in the Soviet Union, has assumed a political as well as ideological character. The U.S. government had declared the "defense of human rights" was becoming a central plank of its foreign policy, and said that it would concentrate its fire on violations of human rights in the communist countries.

Those who have launched this campaign are evidently little embarrassed by the fact that the calls for the defense of human rights in the world come from a country where the sores and evils of contemporary capitalist society manifest themselves in the most exaggerated and ugliest forms.

The debate foisted upon us provides a good opportunity for comparing the socialist and bourgeois ways of life, the real rights and freedoms enjoyed by the working people in the Soviet Union and in the United States. "We have no reason to shun any serious discussion of human rights,"

Leonid Brezhnev said. "Our revolution and the victory of socialism in this country have not only proclaimed but have secured in reality the rights of the working man whatever his nationality, the rights of millions of working people, in a way capitalism has been unable to do in any country of the world.". . .

An important constitutional guarantee of the right of Soviet citizens to the enjoyment of cultural benefits is the extension of cultural exchanges with other countries. True to the commitment made at the Helsinki Conference and proceeding from the interests of satisfying the cultural requirements of the working people, the Party and state encourage in every way cultural exchange by signing appropriate intergovernmental agreements. The USSR maintains cultural contacts with 120 countries.

In the years of Soviet power books by authors from 136 countries have been published in the USSR. The number of titles of these works is 77,500 and the total printing, 2,420 million copies.

According to UNESCO figures, the USSR puts out six times more translated books than Britain, 4.3 times more than the United States, 2.8 times more than Japan, and 2.3 times more than France. Translations of new works by contemporary foreign writers are published in the *Inostrannaya literatura* [Foreign Literature] monthly, which has a circulation of 600,000.

The international ties of the Soviet art world are being steadily extended. Forty large foreign art exhibitions were held in the USSR in 1977–79. They included exhibitions of American paintings from the second half of the nineteenth and twentieth century, pictures from the Georges Pompidou National Art and Culture Center (France), from the collection of the Royal Academy of Arts in London, etc.

At present plays based on more than 130 works by foreign authors are being staged in Soviet theaters. In 1980 alone, the USSR played host to more than 130 foreign theatrical companies and musical groups, which gave over 6,000 performances in more than 170 cities.

Every year the USSR buys and widely shows approximately 60 films from the socialist countries and as many films from capitalist and developing countries. International film festivals are regularly held in our country. In the past few years Soviet TV viewers have seen a number of Western telefilms and serial programs.

It will be noted that films from capitalist countries make up about 10 percent of all films shown in the USSR, while films of all socialist countries account for only five percent of foreign films shown in the West. For example, *The Dawns Are Quiet Here*, which was awarded an honorary Oscar, was barred from the screen in the United States. The film *Liberation*, which has been shown all over the world, was not released for mass showing there either. Films bought by the United States from us are demonstrated in small cinemas, without proper publicity and press reviews. It is no better in the FRG, Italy, and Britain.

It has been said that this happens because readers and film goers in the West are not ready for Soviet literature or films, that they are too serious for them because people in the West are used to another kind of art which abounds in erotic themes and violence.

Are they really? It would be more correct to say that people in the capitalist countries are conditioned to this sort of culture which has come to be called "mass culture." In other words, it is a culture which does not elevate a person to a certain intellectual level, but pushes him down to the lowest level of cultural consumption. Countless detective and spy series, which are full of murder, pornography, and racism, have literally flooded the book market in the West. The same can be said about films. Whom does such "culture" serve? Certainly not the working people. It is a source of enrichment for big publishers and producers, but where ordinary readers and film goers are concerned it arouses base instincts, kills their thoughts, and discourages them from thinking for themselves, including thinking about the problems of remaking society. In the end, "culture" such as this contributes to preserving the positions of monopoly capital.

Naturally, representatives of monopolies in power fear a broadening of cultural contacts with the socialist countries, and they are doing everything to prevent working people in capitalist countries from getting to know about art under socialism. On the other hand, under the guise of cultural exchange, they try to foist upon the socialist countries "wares" that glamorize violence, pornography, racism, acts of aggression, etc. Quite understandably, we are against this kind of "freedom" of cultural exchange. This fully accords with the letter and spirit of the Helsinki Conference. We have never made a secret of the fact that our country welcomes only those works of art which are permeated with the ideas of humanism and democracy and belief in man, and serve to strengthen mutual understanding and trust among nations. . . .

Up to now we have spoken about economic, social, political, and personal rights. Now we shall talk about a right without which all other rights are rendered meaningless. This is the right to live. It means that each person, irrespective of his ideological, political, or religious views, irrespective of the color of his skin and his nationality, has the right to live in peace and be free from the fear of a nuclear catastrophe.

In our country this human right is laid down in the Constitution, as is the obligation of the state and all society to struggle actively for the assertion of this right, for peace.

The imperialists and their mass media, deliberately distorting the essence and meaning of the foreign policy of the Communist Party and the Soviet state, attempt to portray it as a propagandistic cover which hides the allegedly aggressive plans of communism.

But it is clear and understandable to every reasonable person that our peace-loving policy is not a cover, not empty words and declarations. It flows from the very essence of socialism. Lenin always linked together the questions of human rights and democracy with the problems of peace. "Democracy is most clearly manifested," he wrote, "in the fundamental question of war and peace." In actual fact our country does not have a single person who, being interested in war, could stand to gain financially by it, or, shall we say, by the arms race.

The same thing cannot be said about Western countries, especially the United States. Such people do exist there. And although they constitute only a quarter of a percent of the population, they have inestimable wealth and unlimited power concentrated in their hands. The owners of General Dynamics, McDonnell Douglas, Grumman, Boeing, and other firms of the U.S. military-industrial complex live only for war and thrive only on military orders. What does humanity's right to live in peace matter to them!

Marx once quoted in *Capital* a saying which he liked by the English commentator Dunning. Dunning said, about capital, that for 300 percent "there is not a crime at which it will scruple, nor a risk it will not run, even to the chance of its owner being hanged.'' And indeed some military monopolies today receive up to 500 percent pure profit. After this how can one be surprised by the statement made by certain representatives of the military-industrial complex that "there are more important things than peace."

The most reliable criterion of truth is the logic of facts. It shows unmistakably who stands for the preservation of peace and whence comes the threat of a new world war. It shows who is encroaching upon the sacred rights of the nations to live. We shall now turn to the logic of facts. . . .

Our Party has pursued an active struggle for peace since the first days of Soviet power. The Great October Socialist Revolution was victorious under the conditions of the First World War, and the question of withdrawing from this bloody war which had taken ten million lives was important not only to Soviet Russia but also to the workers of other countries. At the Second All-Russia Congress of Soviets, which took place on October 26 (November 8), 1917, a Decree on Peace drawn up by Lenin was adopted, in which it was proposed to the warring nations that they conclude a universal and democratic peace—a peace without annexations and indemnities. This was the first important legislative foreign policy act of the Soviet state. It defined the principles of a policy in international relations which was the first of its type in the history of mankind.

The Entente countries (Britain, France, and so on) and also the United States did not even respond to these proposals. They generally regarded Soviet Russia at that time as some historical anomaly which would not survive for long. But when they saw that the "anomaly" continued to exist, they decided to put an end to it by *mani militari*; in other words, from a position of strength. International imperialism did not want to reconcile itself to the existence of a country where the workers and peasants were in power. In the spring of 1918 American, British, and French troops disembarked at Murmansk; Japanese and, some time later, American and British troops did the same at Vladivostok. The German imperialists seized the western regions of the country. Internal counterrevolution raised its head. The overthrown exploiter classes unleashed a civil war. In the struggle against the Soviet Republic two counterrevolutionary forces joined hands—foreign interventionists and the Russian White Guards.

The Soviet Republic was in an exceptionally difficult situation. The enemy occupied an enormous part of the country. Areas which they had seized were subjected to pillage. The occupationists ferociously did away with patriots defending their Motherland.

The young Soviet state had to make every effort to ward off the attacks of the interventionists and White Guards. For this purpose the Red Army was formed, which, as we well know, honorably fulfilled the task set before it—the task of defending the achievements of socialism.

It is probably appropriate here to recall that it was precisely during the years just after the revolution that the myth about the "Soviet military threat" was born. Lenin wrote in this connection:

> Some foolish people are shouting about red militarism. These are political crooks who pretend that they believe this absurdity and throw charges of this kind right and left, exercising their lawyers' skill in concocting plausible arguments and in throwing dust in the eyes of the masses. . . .
>
> What a "horrible" crime, indeed! The imperialists of the whole world hurled themselves upon the Russian republic in order to crush it, and we began to form an army which for the first time in history knows what it is fighting for . . . and this is denounced as red militarism!

Fighting the imperialists of the whole world single-handed until late 1920, the young, far from strong Soviet state won the battle. Is this a wonder? Yes, but a natural one. "A nation in which the majority are workers and peasants," said Lenin, "realize, feel, and see that they are fighting for their own Soviet power, for the rule of the working people, for the cause whose victory will ensure them and their children all the benefits of culture, of all that has been created by human labor—such a nation can never be vanquished."

Peace was essential for successful socialist construction. Lenin pointed out: "What we prize most is peace and an opportunity to devote all our efforts to restoring our economy." He persistently explained the peace-loving foreign policy of the Soviet state, its interest in the development of economic and cultural relations with all states, first and foremost with the United States. Lenin said, "We are decidedly for an economic understanding with America—with all countries but especially with America. . . . Let the American capitalists leave us alone. We shall not touch them."

Following Lenin's wise directions, the Communist Party and the Soviet state were already at the time persistently coming out in favor of peaceful coexistence between states with different social systems and strove to normalize relations with the capitalists states. At the Genoa conference of European countries in 1922 the Soviet delegation said in its statement: "Taking a viewpoint based on the principles of communism, the Russian delegation recognizes that at the present time, whereby the old social order and the new one which is now being born can exist side by side, economic cooperation between the states representing these two systems of ownership is absolutely imperative." The delegation also brought up a proposal for considering the question of a general reduction in armaments and the banning of the most barbaric methods of waging war—"poisonous gases, aerial combat, and so on, in particular the use of methods of destruction against civilians."

But we did not succeed in reaching an agreement with the Entente powers. The imperialists were not even prepared to consider the question of disarmament. Although they had lost the war against the Soviet republic, the world's bourgeoisie did not abandon their plans for destroying the Soviet system—this time through economic strangulation.

Meanwhile the heroic labor of the Soviet people under the leadership of the Communist Party was yielding results: our country was getting stronger and stronger, its power growing. It was becoming increasingly obvious to the leading circles in the West that the policy of "nonrecognition" of the USSR could not hamper its ability to strengthen itself and its successes. And what is more, this policy was harmful to the capitalist countries themselves. It slowed down the development of economic relations with the Soviet Union, which were of no small advantage to capitalist countries. The blockade ring of nonrecognition crumbled. In 1924 Britain, Austria, Norway, Greece, Sweden, Denmark, Mexico, and France recognized the USSR and established diplomatic relations with it. In 1925 the example of these states was followed by Japan. An important political fact is the establishment in 1933 of diplomatic relations between the USSR and the United States. But it was obvious that such recognition had been forced upon them and that the imperialists had not turned their backs on their plans for the destruction of Soviet power by force of arms.

They refused the USSR any credits, pursued a policy of economic isolation, waged slanderous campaigns, organized acts of sabotage, threatened another military intervention, and continued political provocations.

It is natural that in such a situation the Communist Party and the Soviet government were taking the necessary measures for strengthening the country's defense capability. At the same time, our country, aiming to secure peace, energetically continued the struggle for peace and disarmament. A Preparatory Commission, formed by the League of Nations, for convening a conference on disarmament was used for this purpose. In November 1927 the Soviet government introduced to the Commission a proposal for the complete disarmament of all states. It was rejected. Then in 1928 the USSR introduced a proposal on partial disarmament. The imperialists declined to examine it, too.

But in order to neutralize the impression made on world public opinion by the Soviet peace initiatives, Western propaganda advanced the thesis that they were, allegedly, a tactical ruse on the part of the Bolsheviks, who were "asking" for peace while they were weak, but when they became stronger then they would show their true selves. The imperialists hastened to use their military superiority in order to try yet again to liquidate the Soviet Republic.

Towards the end of 1929 there was an unprecedented economic crisis which caused upheaval in the calculations of the Western powers and cruelly sharpened competition between the imperialist countries for markets and spheres of influence. As had already happened more than once in the past, the ever growing internal difficulties and contradictions compelled them to try and find a way out through adventures in foreign policy, through wars and seizure of foreign territory. A world war became a real threat, again. Those who were most aggressively in favor of a new division of the world were Germany, Italy, and Japan, who were "left out" of the division of territory after the First World War.

In 1931 the Japanese militarists seized Manchuria without a declaration of war, and in 1937 began a war for the seizure of the whole of China.

Particularly dangerous was German imperialism, which had put into power the most reactionary and unrestrained form of capital-fascism in the shape of Hitler's party. In their preparation for war the Nazis armed the country at breakneck speed. In 1936 they sent troops into the Rhine territory and moved right up to the French border. In 1938 they seized Austria.

Fascist Italy, for its part, began to wage a war in 1935 for the capture of Abyssinia (Ethiopia). In 1936 Germany and Italy stirred up the civil war in Spain, having supported the fascist uprising against the republican government.

The flames of war were spreading. The land of the Soviets was threatened both in Europe and in the Far East. The Hitlerites called for a war against the Soviet Union with the aim of "destroying communism." In 1936 Germany and Japan concluded the so-called "Anti-Comintern Pact" which Italy joined a year later. This was a bloc consisting of three aggressors. Under the guise of calling for a "Crusade" against communism, they made speedy preparations for a war to divide up the world. This aggressive bloc was to all intents and purposes directed against the Western powers as well. But they secretly hoped that Hitler and his satellites would satisfy their appetite at the expense of the Soviet Union. In expectation of this they even shut their eyes to the "petty misdemeanors" of the aggressors. In 1938 there came a moment when it seemed that such expectations were justified: the Japanese militarists made an armed attack against the USSR in the Lake Khasan region, and in the summer of the next year they invaded in significant force the territory of the Mongolian People's Republic, with which the Soviet Union was tied by a protocol on mutual assistance. And in both instances the aggressor received a shattering rebuff. By this time the intensive work of the Party and the people yielded tangible results: the defense capability of our country had grown considerably.

At the same time, true to their peace-loving policy, the Communist Party and the Soviet state invariably came out in support of nations which had become the victims of aggression. They spared no efforts to avert the flame of war by setting up a collective security system in Europe. After Germany's seizure of Austria the Soviet Union made a statement in which it proposed an immediate discussion with the other powers in and outside the League of Nations on the appropriate practical measures. "Tomorrow may be too late," the statement said, "but there is still time today if all the states, in particular the great powers, take a firm, clear-cut position in relation to the problem of the collective salvation of the world."

Of course, Hitler would not decide to oppose a coalition comprising the USSR, Britain, France, the United States, and other countries. However, the ruling circles of the Western powers rejected the policy of collective security. As we have already said, they preferred the policy of appeasement of the aggressors, hoping to make a deal with them. They calculated on dragging the USSR into a war with Germany and Japan, while standing to one side and accumulating strength in expectation of the moment when it would be possible to dictate their demands to all three countries ravaged by war. The "model" for this shameful policy of complicity was the Munich Agreement [1938] between France and Britain, on the one hand, and fascist Germany and Italy, on the other, on the dismemberment of Czechoslovakia and the transference of a number of its border territories to Germany. As one should have expected, after a short space of time the Hitlerites seized the whole of Czechoslovakia. In September 1939 Germany attacked Poland. Realizing that their countries' turns had come, the governments of France and Britain declared war on Germany. The Second World War had begun.

The time had come to pay the price for blind anticommunism. France experienced the shame of capitulation and fascist occupation. Britain lived in perpetual fear of Hitler's invading the island. The United States suffered crushing defeats from the Japanese aggressor in the Pacific.

By 1941, having seized many countries in Europe and using their economic resources, fascist Germany invaded the territory of the Soviet Union, without a declaration of war, on June 22, 1941. This was world imperialism's greatest show of strength against socialism. A deadly danger hung over the USSR. The Communist Party, having turned the country into one military camp, rallied and organized the people for the Great Patriotic War.

This unparalleled encounter with a bloody aggressor lasted almost four years. Hitler's Germany was ground into dust. On May 9, 1945, Soviet troops completed their last operation—they smashed a group of the German fascist army surrounding Prague, the capital of Czechoslovakia, and entered the city, already liberated by the people who had risen up against the invaders.

In August 1945 the Soviet army dealt a crushing blow to the armed forces of militarist Japan. On September 2, 1945, Japan signed an act of unconditional surrender. The Soviet Union's Great Patriotic War and the Second World War were over. For the nations of the world the long-awaited peace had come.

As a result of the Second World War a fundamental change took place in the correlation of forces in favor of socialism. Eleven states with a total population of more than seven hundred million broke away from the capitalist system. The time when the USSR was the only country of victorious socialism was at an end.

The reader will have come across the theme of the Great Patriotic War more than once in the preceding chapters. I would like to stress at this point a number of factors, and first and foremost the fact that the USSR carried the main burden of the Second World War on its shoulders. More than 70 percent of Germany's armed forces were at the Soviet-German front. The war brought the Soviet Union enormous casualties: at the front and in fascist captivity more than twenty million Soviet citizens perished. The material damage taken altogether was worth approximately 2,600 billion rubles.* Not a single country in any war had ever known such losses before.

Another factor is that the Second World War was a coalition war. The peoples and armies of the United States, Britain, France, and other countries of the anti-Hitler coalition were fighting against fascist aggression. Troops of Yugoslavia, Poland, Czechoslovakia, Albania, and, after the victory of the national uprisings, Bulgaria and Rumania fought heroically against the fascist plunderers. The members of the Resistance movement in the occupied countries of Europe also made their contribution to the victory over the enemy. The warriors of the Mongolian People's Republic took an active part in smashing the Japanese army. The struggle of the peace-loving peoples from all countries flowed into a single mighty stream.

During the war years the Soviet Union firmly conducted a foreign policy aimed at uniting the antifascist forces. The

---

* At August 1984 exchange rates, 1 ruble equals approximately $1.20.

Teheran conference at the end of 1943 of the heads of government of the USSR, the United States, and Britain played an important role in consolidating the anti-Hitler coalition. It adopted a declaration in which a joint policy for the three Allied powers in the war was formulated and confirmed. Their striving to secure a lasting peace after the war and establish cooperation between all peace-loving countries, large and small, was emphasized.

At the second conference of the leaders from Britain, the United States, and the USSR in the Crimea [Yalta] in February 1945 a plan for Germany's final defeat and the terms for its unconditional surrender were worked out. Basic proposals for the demilitarization and democratization of Germany were accepted at the insistence of the Soviet Union. A statement was made to the effect that it was resolved to establish such guarantees which would not permit Germany to break the peace in the future. With the aim of preserving peace among the nations the conference participants came forward in favor of the formation of the United Nations.

Finally, at the Potsdam conference in July and August 1945, the heads of government of the USSR, the United States, and Britain solemnly pledged themselves to see to it that Germany would never again threaten peace, agreed to do away with German militarism once and for all, to eradicate the Nazi party and not permit it ever to exist again. Moreover, the Soviet delegation firmly defended the just and democratic principles of relations with defeated Germany, thanks to which the plan for its dismemberment, put forward by the United States, was rejected. It was pointed out in the conference decisions that during the occupation Germany was to be regarded by the Allies as a single economic whole, and the supervisory bodies were obliged to conduct a single agreed upon policy. In addition, the Soviet delegation secured the return to Poland of all the territories which had belonged to it since time immemorial; a decision was also reached with regard to its new western borders along the Oder and the Neisse.

The Teheran, Yalta, and Potsdam conferences were convincing proof of the possibilities of cooperation between states with different social systems. We may note that the Soviet Union steadfastly followed the decisions reached by these conferences. One cannot say the same, however, about the other participants.

And one more thing. The lessons of the Great Patriotic War serve as a clea warning to those who are fond of military adventures. The victory of the Soviet Union proved convincingly the vitality and invincibility of the world's first socialist state and the bankruptcy of the plans of the imperialist pretenders to world supremacy.

Those in short are the facts of history. And they categorically bear witness to the fact that ever since it came into being the Soviet Union has always conducted a consistent policy of peace and cooperation between peoples and states. And if the cold winds of the threat of war are blowing over our planet again, then the guilty ones are, as in the past, the sinister forces of imperialism.

Yes, the questions of war and peace, more acute than ever, are again on the agenda of world politics. It is, after all, a well-known fact that the losses of all the participants in the Second World War together (50 million people) cannot be compared with what atomic war would bring.

If one judges by some outward signs, then one can come to the conclusion that we have returned again to the situation which preceded the Second World War. But those are only outward signs. The situation now has fundamentally changed. There is no denying that imperialism, as before, is the source which breeds all wars. But now there are forces in the world capable of sobering up any aggressor and averting a catastrophe. These forces are concentrated around the world socialist system headed by the Soviet Union. That is why the sacred right of the people to life is no longer merely a beautiful dream but a reality. Peace can be preserved today. But under one immutable condition: all the peoples must actively fight for it. . . .

Two opposing courses in international politics—socialist and imperialist—were preserved after the Second World War as well.

The Soviet people, under the leadership of the Communist Party, set about peaceful constructive labor. All their strength was put into restoring and developing the country's national economy. Domestic and foreign policies were subordinated to solving these tasks. The main aims of the Party's foreign policy were the ensuring of a stable and lasting peace, the consolidation of socialism's position in the world arena, the assistance to those nations which had broken away from capitalism, and the building of a new life.

Events in the capitalist world took a different direction. As though led by the force of inertia, the imperialists again returned to the policy of military threats and blackmail. The United States of America became the main center of reaction which had sharply increased its economic and military potential. In August 1945, towards the end of the war, American planes dropped atomic bombs on Hiroshima and Nagasaki. The tragedy of these Japanese cities can in no way be justified. The U.S. government's act was dictated not by military necessity, as some people try to claim, but merely by a desire to demonstrate that they possessed nuclear power, to frighten the peoples of the world and put pressure on the USSR with regard to solving postwar problems.

In pursuit of world supremacy, the U.S. ruling circles openly declared that their aims could be achieved only from a position of strength, and waged the so-called cold war. At their initiative the aggressive bloc of imperialist countries was formed in 1949 under the name of the North Atlantic Treaty Organization (NATO). On a scale hitherto unknown, the United States expanded the arms race and began to step up the production of atomic, thermonuclear, bacteriological weapons and other types of mass destruction weapons. American military bases, targeted on the USSR and other socialist countries, were being quickly set up; new military blocs were being formed. In various parts of Europe and Asia dangerous hotbeds of tension sprung up.

The CPSU and the Soviet government could not ignore the dangerous course of American imperialism, which had the atomic weapons at its disposal, and openly proclaimed its intention to achieve the "rolling back" of socialism. We had constantly to build up the USSR's defense capability. The fact that the Soviet Union came into possession of atomic, and later thermonuclear, weapons and mastered the production of intercontinental missiles, which put an end to U.S. atomic blackmail, is of immense principled significance. In May 1955 in Warsaw the USSR and the European states of the people's democracy signed a Treaty of Friendship, Cooperation, and Mutual Assistance, which became an important stabilizing factor in Europe. These answering measures of a legitimate defensive nature were described by Western propaganda as a growing military threat from the Soviet Union and the socialist community as a whole. Meanwhile, our growing strength acts not as a means for attacking other countries, not for encroaching upon another's property or territory. Our strength acts as a guarantee of peaceful labor, a better life for the Soviet people, and the defense of their political, social, and economic achievements. Merely this and nothing more. That is why we are always ready—and we have proposed this more than once—to cut military expenditures and ban weapons of mass destruction, and any other weapons all the way to complete and general disarmament. But on one indisputable condition: that the Western powers do the same.

War is not our policy, and we adopted a law 30 years ago which makes propaganda of war a serious crime. This statute is included in the Constitution of the USSR. There are no such statutes in any constitution in the West.

The consistently peace-loving foreign policy of the USSR has invariably been reaffirmed in the decisions of our Party congresses. The Twentieth CPSU Congress (1956), in setting out the Soviet government's foreign policy tasks, spoke of the need for improving relations with the capitalist countries and consistently carrying out the Leninist policy of peaceful coexistence between states with different social systems; it drew the theoretical conclusion that it was feasible to avert a world war in the present international situation. The Twenty-second Congress (1961) emphasized once again the necessity to adhere firmly to the principle of peaceful coexistence. It called for vigorously exposing the intrigues and maneuvers of the imperialist war mongers and strengthening world peace. The foreign policy of the Soviet state, it was stated in a resolution of the Twenty-third Congress (1966), aims to defend consistently the principle of peaceful coexistence between states with different social systems, to give a decisive rebuff to the aggressive imperialist forces, and to save mankind from a new world war.

As in the years preceding the Second World War, the Soviet Communist Party regarded general and complete disarmament as a radical way of consolidating peace, along with setting up a collective security system which would call for joint peaceful efforts on the part of states situated in one or other region of the world.

Europe was of particular significance in this respect. There the grim legacy of the Second World War was still to be felt; the German question had not been settled, while in the Federal Republic of Germany militarist and revenge-seeking tendencies were growing, and the army (the Bundeswehr) had become one of the most powerful in Western Europe. Its strength regained, German imperialism was reaching for the atomic weapons, seeking a revision of the results of the Second World War and laying claims to the German Democratic Republic and West Berlin.

On other continents too a situation dangerous to the cause of peace prevailed. The deepening of the general crisis of capitalism was accompanied by the increased activities of the forces of imperialist reaction, first and foremost the United States, by intensified subversive activities against and interference in the internal affairs of countries which had taken the road to social progress. In the summer of 1962 a real danger arose of an attack on Cuba by the American militarists. In 1965 the United States unleashed an armed intervention in South Vietnam, and extended its military actions to the Democratic Republic of Vietnam. In the summer of 1967 the ruling circles of Israel, with the support of the American and other imperialists, launched aggression against the United Arab Republic (Egypt), Syria, and Jordan, and seized large areas of Arab territory. A serious threat to peace and the independence of the nations was also growing in other parts of Asia, Africa, and Latin America.

In that situation the Soviet Union and other socialist countries made persistent efforts to consolidate peace in Europe and liquidate the consequences of the Second World War. As far back as 1954 the Soviet government proposed to the European countries and the United States a plan for a European agreement on collective security. The Western powers, however, refused to accept it, just like other similar proposals which were made over subsequent years. One of them, made in 1966, was the proposal by the Political Consultative Committee of the Warsaw Treaty member states for holding a European conference to discuss questions relating to setting up a collective security system and establishing good-neighborly relations in Europe.

The Soviet Union put forward a series of initiatives aimed at solving the problem of disarmament stage by stage, and above all, restraining the arms race. It advanced many proposals in different years concerning a reduction of conventional weapons and armed forces of the great powers; a ban on nuclear weapons and a stop to nuclear tests; the establishment of nuclear-free zones; the freezing of the military budgets of all states; the withdrawal of foreign troops from the territories of other countries; the conclusion of a non-aggression treaty between the NATO and Warsaw Treaty countries; the working-out of measures to reduce the danger of a surprise attack; the establishment of a strict control over disarmament; the prohibition of war propaganda, and so on.

The Soviet Union corroborated its peace-loving policy with practical actions. It reduced its armed forces to the 1939 level and then twice more, in 1955 and 1960, it made a further significant reduction on a unilateral basis. In 1958 it stated it would terminate atomic and hydrogen weapons tests in the atmosphere, provided the other countries possessing these weapons took similar measures. To facilitate the reaching of an agreement on disarmament, the Soviet Union met the Western powers halfway more than once by accepting their proposals. But as soon as it took such a step, the initiators of these proposals renounced their own declarations or suggested such measures, the implementation of which would ensure their military superiority over the USSR. Using their rhetoric on disarmament as a camouflage, they deceived the nations and continued the arms race, all the while conducting the cold war policy as persistently as ever.

And yet the Soviet Union's efforts were not in vain. Like seeds falling on fertile soil, they produced vigorous shoots. World public opinion was that soil. As Lenin, the founder of our state, once said, "We must show the significance of communism in practice, by example." The force of the example, initially, of the first socialist country, and then of the whole socialist community has always been and continues to be demonstrated precisely in questions of war and peace. In recent decades, more and more people throughout the world have been rising in their millions to participate actively in political affairs. And they realize with increasing clarity who is fighting for mankind's right to live and who wants to deprive it of this right. And even those who do not yet accept socialist ideals are beginning to understand that their hopes for preserving peace and averting a nuclear catastrophe coincide with the will of socialism for peace. This, apart from everything else, is the new factor which distinguishes today's situation in the world from that of the prewar period of the 1930s. This is why the CPSU has attached special significance to the unity of all peace-loving forces throughout the world in the struggle for peace and the prevention of a new world war and why it has made its own enormous contribution to this truly historical movement and is continuing to do so. The international conferences of the Communist and Workers' Parties of 1957, 1960, and 1969 have played an important role here.

The participants in the 1957 conference—and they represented parties from 64 countries—adopted the program documents: the Declaration and Manifesto of Peace. The declaration proclaimed the struggle for peace, against the imperialists' war preparations, as the most important international task of the Communists. "Peace," said the Manifesto, "can be preserved only if all to whom it is dear combine their forces, sharpen their vigilance in relation to the machinations of the war instigators, and become fully conscious that their sacred duty is to intensify the struggle for peace, which is threatened."

At the 1960 Conference representatives from 81 parties unanimously adopted a Statement and Appeal to the Peoples of the World. These documents developed and enriched the ideas of the 1957 Declaration and Manifesto of Peace and outlined a comprehensive program for a decisive, purposeful struggle of the nations against the threat of a new world war. "The Communists," the statement emphasized, "regard it as their historical mission not only to abolish exploitation and poverty on a world scale and rule out for all time the possibility of war of any kind in the life of human society, but also to deliver mankind from the nightmare of a new world war already in our time."

At the 1969 International Conference delegations from 75 Communist and Workers' Parties adopted documents expounding the specific tasks of the anti-imperialist forces on all continents, and emphasizing the need for their unity and more vigorous efforts to defend peace, avert the danger of war, and prevent a world thermonuclear conflagration.

The concerted and decisive actions of the Communist and Workers' Parties served as a powerful impulse for the development in the 1960s of a large-scale movement for peace and a relaxation of international tension.

It will be no exaggeration to say that as they entered the 1970s, the peace-loving forces of the world pinned their hopes on the USSR. Their hopes and aspirations were expressed by the Twenty-fourth CPSU Congress, which put forward a Program of struggle for peace and international cooperation, for the freedom and independence of the peoples. This Program set out the following tasks:

1. To eliminate the hotbeds of war in Southeast Asia and in the Middle East and to promote a political settlement in these areas on the basis of respect for the legitimate rights of states and peoples subjected to aggression. To give an immediate and firm rebuff to any acts of aggression and international arbitrariness. For this, full use must also be made of the possibilities of the United Nations. Repudiation of the threat or use of force in settling outstanding issues must become a law of international life. For its part, the Soviet Union invites the countries which accept this approach to conclude appropriate bilateral or regional treaties.

2. To proceed from the final recognition of the territorial changes that took place in Europe as a result of the Second World War. To bring about a radical mental turn towards détente and peace on this continent. To ensure the convocation and success of a European conference. To do everything to ensure collective security in Europe. We reaffirm the readiness expressed jointly by the defensive Warsaw Treaty member-states, to undertake the simultaneous dissolution of the Warsaw Treaty and the North Atlantic alliance or, as a first step, the liquidation of their military organizations.

3. To conclude agreements banning nuclear, chemical, and bacteriological weapons. To put an end to all nuclear weapons tests, including underground tests, by everyone everywhere. To promote the establishment of nuclear-free zones in various parts of the world. The Soviet Union stands for the nuclear disarmament of all states possessing nuclear weapons, and for the convocation for these purposes of a conference of the five nuclear powers: the USSR, the United States, the People's Republic of China, France, and Britain.

4. To invigorate the struggle to halt the race in all types of weapons. The Soviet Union has suggested convening a worldwide conference for examining questions of disarmament to their full extent; for liquidating foreign military bases; for reducing armed forces and armaments in areas where military confrontation is especially dangerous, first and foremost, in Central Europe; and for working out measures reducing the probability of accidental outbreak or deliberate fabrication of armed incidents and their development into international crises, into war. The Soviet Union expresses readiness to negotiate agreements on reducing military expenditure, above all by the major powers.

5. To carry out in full the UN decisions on the abolition of the remaining colonial regimes. To subject to universal condemnation and boycott all manifestations of racism and apartheid.

6. To extend relations of mutually advantageous cooperation in all spheres with states who for their part seek to do so; to participate with them in solving such problems as environmental protection, development of power and other natural resources, development of transport and communications, prevention and eradication of the most dangerous and widespread diseases, and the exploration and development of outer space and the world ocean.

Putting into practice the Peace Program put forward by the Twenty-fourth Congress, the Communist Party and the Soviet government made a major contribution to social progress on the international arena and promoted the historical turn in international relations from the cold war to peaceful coexistence of states with different social systems. The imperialist circles in the West could not but take into account the growing might of the Soviet Union and the socialist community as a whole. Sober-minded politicians in the capitalist countries gradually came to recognize that the relaxation of international tension was not a whim but an objective and urgent necessity. A period of easing of tension and development of fruitful cooperation had begun. The peoples of the world could breathe more easily. The sacred right to life was gaining a stronger foothold. Thus the increased might of socialism not only posed no threat of any kind, as the shortsighted soothsayers of imperialism predicted, but, on the contrary, became a decisive factor in improving the international climate.

The new period was subsequently characterized by the meaningful word "détente," a word which became part of the vocabularies of all nations.

Détente and the changes it had brought forth in international relations gave rise to certain discussions in the world which are still going on. One argument often voiced in the West is that détente is a "one-way street"; that is, a process which, allegedly, benefits only socialism. In actual fact this claim has nothing in common with reality. Détente has indeed brought benefits—and really substantial ones—to all nations of the world. There is no nation which could have suffered harm from the consolidation of the foundations of Euopean security, the lowering of the level of international tension, the development of mutually advantageous cooperation between states belonging to opposing social systems, or from extending contacts between people in different countries.

Of course, a fact is a fact: it was confirmed with absolute clarity during the period of détente that the climate which it had brought about is especially beneficial to those who work for peace and friendship between nations, for their freedom. On the other hand, it became particularly obvious that the climate of détente and the consolidation of peace is harmful to the "health" of those who enrich themselves by the arms race and link their well-being with the oppression of other nations. In other words, the period of détente was fresh confirmation that the interests of imperialism and those of the peoples diverge and are in irreconcilable conflict with one another, while the interests of mankind and the cause of peace and the interests of socialism and social progress completely coincide.

That is why it is not surprising that during the period of détente, thanks to their unity, solidarity, and mutual support, the countries of socialism were able to solve a number of important tasks ensuring the consolidation of the positions of world socialism. The heroic people of Vietnam gained a glorious victory in defending their independence and socialist achievements. The peoples of Laos and Cambodia (Kampuchea) won their freedom. The seat of war was extinguished in Indochina. In Europe, an outstanding result of the joint efforts of the countries of socialism was the universal recognition of the German Democratic Republic, its admission to the UN, and the reaffirmation on an international level of the inviolability of the western borders of the German Democratic Republic, Poland, and Czechoslovakia. Socialism had firmly asserted itself on Cuban soil. Imperialism's economic and diplomatic blockade of the republic of Cuba had not achieved its purpose.

While fulfilling the Peace Program, the USSR was consistently strengthening its relations with countries freed from colonial dependence. A good deal of attention was given to reaching a just political settlement in the Middle East, rendering support to the Arab peoples in their struggle to abolish the results of Israeli aggression and create a sovereign state of the Palestinian peoples, deprived of their legitimate rights. Political, material, and moral support was given to the peoples of the former Portuguese colonies in Africa who had established independent states (Angola, Mozambique). The Soviet Union signed bilateral treaties of friendship and cooperation with many countries in Asia and Africa and rendered major assistance to newly free countries in strengthening their political and economic independence.

Where its relations with the capitalist countries are concerned, in implementing the Peace Program, the Soviet Union consistently struggled to establish the principles of peaceful coexistence for reducing and eventually eliminating the danger of a new world war. And significant progress had been made to this end. There was a successful development in our relations with France, which was one of the first Western powers to enter into extensive cooperation with the USSR. The Principles of Cooperation, signed between the USSR and France in 1971, laid a longterm foundation for Soviet-French relations. Relations with the Federal Republic of Germany continued developing on the basis of the Moscow Agreement, concluded in 1971 and put into effect in 1972, and important agreements on developing bilateral cooperation were signed. After lengthy negotiations, the initiator of which was the Soviet Union, the USSR, the United States, Britain, and France signed an agreement on West Berlin, which significantly decreased tension in Europe. The policy of peaceful coexistence was gathering momentum.

All this subsequently bore tangible results, which served the common good. Thus, from 1976 to 1980 the volume of trade between the USSR and France had tripled, and between the USSR and Federal Republic of Germany it had doubled; Soviet-French contacts in the fields of science, technology, and culture developed along more than 300 lines; a number of important projects were jointly carried out by the USSR and the FRG. Cooperation with Italy in the economic and cultural spheres was improved. After a break of 40 years, relations with Spain were normalized. Soviet-Finnish relations continued to develop on a firm basis of good-neighborliness.

A change for the better in the Soviet Union's relations with the United States was of decisive significance in reducing the threat of a new world war and consolidating peace. The Party Central Committee devoted special attention to this question. During the summit talks in 1972, 1973, and 1974 important agreements and documents were signed, including the Basic Principles of Mutual Relations between the Soviet Union and the United States; agreements on the limitation of antiballistic missile systems; on the limitation of underground nuclear weapons tests; on the prevention of a nuclear war; on cooperation in the exploration and use of outer space for peaceful purposes; agreements on cooperation in the fields of science and technology; agreements on trade; on the prevention of incidents on and over the high seas. The document entitled Basic Principles of Negotiations for the Further Limitation of Offensive Strategic Arms was also signed. Both sides agreed to work out an agreement on the limitation of offensive strategic arms, to last through 1985, which would be based on the principles of equality and equal security. All this served the improvement in Soviet-American relations and promoted a further relaxation in international tension.

One of the most important events in the history of international relations was the Conference on Security and Cooperation in Europe, which completed its work in Helsinki in the middle of 1975. The path to the Conference was not an easy one. It had required much effort from the Communist Party, the Soviet government, and the fraternal parties of socialist countries; opposition from the forces of militarism and reaction had to be overcome. The most high-ranking political and government leaders from 33 countries, as well as from the United States and Canada, signed the Final Act which, both in letter and spirit, fully satisfied the demands of peaceful coexistence.

The Declaration on Principles Guiding Relations Between Participating States was an integral part of the Final Act. It proclaimed the principles of the sovereign equality of states and their sovereign rights, including the right to choose freely and develop their own political, social, and cultural systems; the nonuse of force or threat of force; the inviolability of existing borders; the territorial integrity of states; peaceful settlement of disputes; noninterference in the internal affairs of one another; respect for human rights and fundamental freedoms; the equality of all peoples and their right to be masters of their own destinies; cooperation between states; and the conscientious fulfillment of obligations according to international law.

A significant part of the Final Act was devoted to questions of extending and invigorating cooperation between the European states in economy, science, technology, environmental protection, and other areas, and also to questions of cultural, educational, and informational exchanges and of establishing contacts between people. The Document on Confidence-Building Measures and Certain Aspects of Security and Disarmament outlined accords which were aimed at reducing the danger of armed conflicts. In particular, it provided for advance notification of large-scale military maneuvers and large-scale movements of troops, the mutual exchange of observers, and certain other measures.

The Helsinki meeting, unprecedented in history, became an event of immense international significance. It was precisely this meeting which introduced the word "détente" into the international lexicon. But however great the significance of the Helsinki meeting, the important thing was to put its collective decisions into effect. "We proceed," observed Leonid Brezhnev, "from the assumption that all countries represented at the Conference will carry out the agreements which have been reached. As far as the Soviet Union is concerned, it will do precisely that."

Now the pressing problem was that of military relaxation, which had to be solved if much that had been achieved was to be more than good intentions. The question was put in precisely this way by the Twenty-fifth Congress of the CPSU, which drew the attention of the world public to the necessity of taking concrete measures in the field of disarmament. The Congress called for a stop to the mounting arms race, a reduction in the accumulated stockpiles of arms, and consistent disarmament. With these aims in mind it was proposed that preparations for a new agreement between the USSR and the United States on the limitation and reduction of strategic arms be speeded up and efforts be made to invigorate the talks on the reduction of armed forces and armaments in Central Europe, which had begun in Vienna in 1973.

Emphasis was also made on the vital importance of concluding as quickly as possible agreements on a universal and complete stop to nuclear weapon tests, a ban on the production of new types and systems of weapons of mass destruction, and on the prohibition of military or any other hostile use of environmental modification techniques. The Congress called for introducing an international practice of systematic reductions of military expenditures, for fresh efforts to convene as soon as possible a world conference on disarmament, and conclude a world agreement on nonuse of force in international relations.

The Party regarded these and other problems as a direct continuation and development of the Peace Program put forward by the Twenty-fourth CPSU Congress, as a program for the further struggle for peace and international cooperation and for the freedom and independence of the nations. The foreign policy of the CPSU and the Soviet government was directed toward solving these problems and achieving the further easing of international tension.

While implementing the Program, the USSR continued actively to pursue the Leninist policy of peaceful coexistence and mutually advantageous cooperation with capitalist countries and giving a firm rebuff to aggressive imperialist intrigues. At that stage peaceful cooperation between countries representing the two systems on the European continent was on the whole developing fairly satisfactorily, despite the efforts of the enemies of détente. Political contacts became more extensive and fruitful. Economic, scientific, and technological ties had also broadened and acquired new qualities. Multilateral measures had been carried out with regard to various questions of European cooperation and serious steps taken to promote military relaxation.

The immense amount of work which had been put into drafting the Treaty between the USSR and the United States on the Limitation of Strategic Offensive Arms was complete when it was signed in 1979 as a result of the summit meeting at Vienna. Much had been done during negotiations with the United States and Britain on the total prohibition of nuclear weapons tests. A convention came into force which prohibits modification of the environment for military purposes. Preliminary agreement was reached on the basic clauses of a treaty prohibiting radiological weapons. Negotiations on the elimination of chemical weapons from the arsenals of all states continued, although inadmissibly slowly. Plans for the deployment of the neutron weapon in Western Europe were successfully held in check.

Many important initiatives, which the Soviet Union and its allies put forward after the Party's Twenty-fifth Congress, were approved in UN resolutions and also by the Special Session of the General Assembly on Disarmament.

On the whole the 1970s saw a substantial improvement in the international climate as a result of, first and foremost, the many-sided and active work on the part of the countries of the socialist community, which relied on the growth in the economic and defensive might of socialism. In the process of détente peaceful coexistence between states with different social systems was consolidated and began to acquire concrete economic and political substance. There was an evident

abatement of the cold war, and favorable objective precon-
ditions matured for settling controversies and international
conflicts by just, peaceful means.

It seemed that before all the people of the world the
possibility of looking to the future with confidence and hope
had at last opened up. Unfortunately, however, it turned out
to be otherwise. Already in the second half of the 1970s the
world situation had begun to deteriorate once more and
become aggravated.

Was this unexpected? Not at all. At the moment when
détente was flourishing, Leonid Brezhnev, the head of the
Soviet delegation, said at the Conference on Security and
Cooperation in Europe that détente could encounter stormy
weather, that all participating states had to make joint efforts
and work on a day-to-day basis to broaden détente. Barely
three months had passed when our head of state was forced
to make the observation that "the opponents of détente and
disarmament are not laying down their arms. By various
means they are trying to sow distrust and hostility between
states, dragging the nations back to the days of the 'cold war'
and calling for the accumulation of more and more stockpiles
of weapons that are even more destructive."

In other words, the aggressive forces have continued to
exist and work actively even in the years of détente. Not
wishing to come to terms with present-day realities, which
came about not as a result of anyone's malevolence, but as a
result of the objective laws of social development coming into
play, these forces resorted to action in the latter half of the
1970s. One can formulate their aim in this way: they attempted
to stop the wheel of history with the help of force.

Never before in peacetime have the imperialist states
carried out such a quantitative buildup and qualitative improvement in the conventional and strategic types of weapons
as at the beginning of the 1980s. It is envisaged, moreover,
that such a buildup in military potential will continue almost
to the end of the present century. And at the same time,
never before have imperialism's mass media embarked upon
such a huge campaign of spreading the myth of "Soviet
threat."

It must be said here that no one has or is able to come
up with any proof of the presence of a military threat from
the Soviet Union. And it is understandable because there has

not been nor is any threat from the Soviet Union. Our military doctrine, as we have stated quite officially on several occasions, is of a consistently defensive character. We are opponents of aggressive wars. We decisively reject the concept of a "first strike," a "preventive war" and so on. All our defensive measures are intended exclusively to counter the threat created by the arms race in the West. And we are implementing these measures in such a way as to not upset the existing balance of forces and to preserve the equilibrium. We do not seek military superiority.

In an attempt to prove their statements on the "Soviet threat," our opponents sometimes advance this argument: since the Russians consider that in the final analysis communism must be victorious throughout the world, they are consequently nurturing aggressive designs in relation to other countries. Toward the end of January 1981 this accusation was made in the United States at the highest official level. It was stated that the Soviet Union, allegedly, intends to "create a universal socialist or communist state."

This, however, is a lie from start to finish. Our country has never set, nor could it set itself such aims. Communists in general—and Soviet communists in particular—consider that in the final analysis socialism will be victorious throughout the world. But this is a matter of the objective course of history. It will come about as a result of the will of the peoples of the appropriate countries themselves and not as a result of the so-called export of revolution. We have always considered and still consider that it is impossible to make any revolution a reality by artificial means. Lenin said that the theory of "pushing" revolutions would mean a complete break with Marxism, which always rejected the "pushing" of revolutions, for they develop as the class contradictions giving birth to revolution grow more acute. The leadership of our Party fully shares this view today. It may be recalled that Leonid Brezhnev stated at the Twenty-sixth Congress of the CPSU: "We are against the export of revolution, and we cannot agree to any export of counterrevolution either." Our views on the aforementioned problem have not changed in any way and no one in our country has intended or intends to export revolution.

Incidentally, many prominent spokesmen for Western public opinion acknowledge this fact and state directly that the social changes taking place in the world are caused not by Soviet interference, but by social injustice, oppression, poverty, and destitution.

Nevertheless, the campaign around the "Soviet threat" continues. And it is accompanied by statements on the inevitability, and even necessity, of war.

When the process of détente began to slow down, when confrontation was growing, all people throughout the world were waiting to see how the Soviet Union would react. And then the whole world heard once again the calm and businesslike voice of the Soviet Communists, who gave from the rostrum of their Twenty-sixth Congress a clear and sober analysis of the existing situation in the world:

> Adventurism, and a readiness to gamble with the vital interests of humanity for narrow and selfish ends—this is what has emerged in a particularly barefaced form in the policy of the more aggressive imperialist circles. . . . Indeed, they have set out to achieve the unachievable—to set up a barrier to progressive changes in the world and to again become the rulers of the peoples' destinies.

In the complex international situation the Communist Party and the Soviet state have shown genuinely Leninist self-possession, firmness, and adherence to principle, defending and putting into practice a course of peace, not yielding to provocations, and at the same time giving a firm rebuff to imperialist claims.

The Twenty-sixth Congress of the CPSU put forward a set of new, major, and realistic proposals representing an organic continuation and development of the Peace Program proclaimed by the Twenty-fourth and Twenty-fifth Party Congresses, as applied to the most vital and pressing problems of today. They involve the central problems of international relations and include measures both of a political and a military nature. These proposals make provision for broadening the zones where confidence-building measures of a military nature can be applied; the readiness of the Soviet Union to continue without delay negotiations with the United States on the limitation and reduction of strategic arms, while preserving all the positive elements that have so far been achieved in this area; reaching an agreement with the United States on limiting the deployment of new types of weapons; establishing a moratorium on the deployment in Europe of new medium-range nuclear missile weapons of the NATO countries and the Soviet Union; and many other measures, which should have a positive effect on the easing of international tension.

The Congress paid special attention to the necessity of putting an immediate stop to a new round of the arms race, because the qualitatively new types of weapons being developed can make it exceptionally difficult, if not simply impossible, to establish control over them. The U.S. doctrine of a "limited" nuclear war through which it is being suggested to world public opinion that the devil is not so black as he is painted was decisively exposed. "But that is sheer deception of the peoples! A 'limited' nuclear war as conceived by the Americans in, say, Europe would from the outset mean the certain destruction of European civilization. And of course the United States, too, would not be able to escape the flames of war."

We Communists are always trying to influence people by means of persuasion and our Twenty-sixth Congress is a new proof of that. However, for those who are unaffected by the method of persuasion, it served as a very serious warning. In the report to the Congress it was said:

> We would like to hope, however, that those who shape United States policy today will ultimately manage to see things in a more realistic light. The military and strategic equilibrium prevailing between the USSR and the U.S., between the Warsaw Treaty [member-states] and NATO, objectively serves to safeguard world peace. We have not sought, and do not now seek, military superiority over the other side. That is not our policy. But neither will we permit the building up of any such superiority over us. Attempts of that kind and talking to us from a position of strength are absolutely futile.

So is it not better to keep one's feet on realistic ground and talk about the prospects for peace and not war? But the main thing is not just to talk but to do everything possible to consolidate peace.

During the period after the Twenty-sixth Congress the world public could see for itself again and again that our Party's words are not divorced from deeds. The Soviet Union, acting consistently and with persistence, backs the provisions of the Peace Program for the 1980s with concrete initiatives, aiming to defuse the threat of war, consolidate peace, and deepen détente. These initiatives include the USSR's reaffirmation that it will never use nuclear weapons against those states which refuse to produce and use them and do not have them on their territory. The Soviet Union has also expressed a readiness to do everything possible to achieve a speedy and constructive result at the Geneva talks on medium-range nuclear weapons; to resume without delay, Soviet-American talks on the limitation and reduction of strategic nuclear weapons and on the limitation of military activity in the Indian Ocean and later in the Pacific Ocean; to ratify at any moment the 1974 treaty on the limitation of underground nuclear weapon tests; to agree on putting an end not only to all nuclear weapons tests but also to the further production of nuclear weapons; the reduction and eventually the complete liquidation of military nuclear stockpiles; to examine without prejudice all proposals made by the other side on disarmament, proceeding from the degree to which they are equal to the task of averting war and consolidating peace and correspond to the principle of equality and equal security.

The realistic and constructive approach of the land of the October Revolution to the cardinal international problems of today has been conclusively expressed in Leonid Brezhnev's speech at the Seventeenth Soviet Trade Unions' Congress. With the intention of making it easier to reach a just agreement on a major reduction in the nuclear weapons of both sides in Europe, the Soviet leadership adopted a decision to introduce on a unilateral basis a moratorium on the deployment of medium-range nuclear weapons in the European part of the USSR. Our country is already putting a freeze on such weapons which have already been developed there both qualitatively and quantitatively. This moratorium will be in force until an agreement with the United States is reached on the reduction of medium-range nuclear weapons, which have been designated for [placement in] Europe, on the basis of equality and equal security, or until the U.S. leaders, in disregard for the security of the nations, proceed toward actual preparations for the deployment of Pershing II and cruise missiles in Europe. Demonstrating its will for peace, the Soviet Union, on its own initiative, intends to reduce in 1982 the number of its medium-range missiles, provided of course there is no new aggravation in the international situation.

In June 1982, on behalf of the 269 million Soviet people, Leonid Brezhnev addressed the Second Special Session of the UN General Assembly on Disarmament with a message in which he said in particular:

> Guided by a desire to do all in its power to deliver the peoples from the threat of nuclear devastation and ultimately to exclude its very possibility from the life of mankind, the Soviet state solemnly declares:
>
> The Union of Soviet Socialist Republics assumes an obligation not to be the first to use nuclear weapons.
>
> The commitment shall become effective immediately, the moment it is made public from the rostrum of the UN General Assembly.

It is quite obvious that if it depended on the Soviet Union alone, there would be no nuclear weapons on earth, there would be no development of ever-new methods of mass destruction and nothing would threaten mankind's supreme right—the right to live in peace. We may note in this connection that in the postwar period the USSR has put forward more than 100 proposals designed to put a break on and reverse the production of weapons of destruction and death. As many times the United States has brushed aside these proposals.

The United States hastened to brush aside the new Soviet peace initiatives as well, having declared that there is nothing new or substantial in them. However, we are not living in the 1930s or 1950s, or even the 1960s. It is simply impossible to brush aside peace proposals today because they enjoy the fervent support of the peoples of the capitalist countries themselves. It would be no mistake to say that the early 1980s will go down in history as the beginning of a truly popular struggle for peace, for the right to life. The movement of the peoples of Scandinavian countries for the creation of a nuclear-free zone in the north of Europe and for the complete liquidation of nuclear weapons on the European continent, the movement of hundreds of thousands of Britons against the deployment in Britain of the new U.S. nuclear missiles, the antiwar movement in West Germany under the slogan "No to Pershing and cruise missiles!", the peace marches of thousands of people in Switzerland, the Netherlands, Belgium, and Denmark, important antiwar actions in India, Japan, and many other countries in Asia, Africa, and Latin America—this was how world public opinion responded to the U. S.

rejection of Soviet peace initiatives and those who consider that there are more important things than peace. And what is most gratifying is the fact that people are not waiting for peace to be handed to them on a plate, they are becoming more and more aware that if you want peace you must fight for it. And this is what they are doing.

Certain bourgeois propaganda organs hastened to announce that the peace demonstrations, unprecedented in scale, were the work of the "hand of Moscow." And they made fools of themselves because by this they acknowledged the force and reality of socialism, which, by its indefatigable and consistent struggle for peace, and by the force of its example, has infected hundreds of millions throughout the world. And we Communists can only be proud of this. If what is implied by the talk about the "hand of Moscow" is interference in the internal affairs of the Western world, then it is nothing but an absurdity. The right to life cannot be anyone's internal affair. It is indeed a global problem, the prerogative of mankind as a whole. This was also acknowledged by the UN Commission on Human Rights, which adopted in Geneva a resolution on the need to ensure the right to life—the most vital and inalienable right of each person. This resolution, the draft of which was put forward, incidentally, again on the initiative of the Soviet Union and several other socialist and developing countries, expressed the conviction that "for each nation of the world there is not a single question now more important than the preservation of peace and the assurance of the first and foremost right of each person—the right to life." In the document it is pointed out that it is necessary for the international community to make efforts with the aim of preserving peace, eliminating the threat of nuclear war, and curbing the arms race. The overwhelming majority of delegations expressed their support for this important initiative. Stubborn opposition to approving the resolution was shown only by the United States and its closest allies.

Following Europe and other continents a powerful movement against the intensifying arms race has also developed in the United States itself. A very broad cross section of American society—workers, religious and political figures, students, businessmen—are joining in the struggle for peace. According to one Gallup poll, more than 70 percent of Americans polled were in favor of a U.S.-USSR agreement on stopping the production of new nuclear weapons.

This has nothing to do with the "hand of Moscow," but with the fact that the overwhelming majority of the people in the West itself consider the policy of the representatives of military imperialist monopolies in power to be antipopular and incompatible with the interests of man and humaneness. What does their policy have to do with democracy and democratic rights?

As far as the Soviet Union is concerned, there is not and cannot be such a gap between the leadership's views and the stand of the whole people. The Soviet people unanimously support the foreign policy course of the CPSU. The struggle for peace, consolidation of the security of the peoples, and broad international cooperation has become a truly national cause in our country. It is being actively pursued by the trade unions, the Young Communist League, and other public organizations.

The Soviet Peace Committee, the Soviet Peace Fund, the Union of Soviet Societies of Friendship and Cultural Relations with Foreign Countries, the Committee of Youth Organizations of the USSR, the Soviet Women's Committee, the Soviet War Veterans' Committee, the Soviet Afro-Asian Solidarity Committee, and the Soviet Committee for European Security and Cooperation have made great contributions to this struggle.

Take, for example, the Union of Soviet Societies of Friendship and Cultural Relations with Foreign Countries. This mass public organization aims to promote mutual understanding, friendship, and cooperation between the peoples of the USSR and other countries. It unites 77 Soviet associations and societies of friendship with individual countries and groups of countries and 14 republican friendship societies and local branches in several cities in the Russian Federation.* Thirteen associations and sections for scientific and cultural figures and an Association of Twin Cities are also members of the Union of Soviet Societies of Friendship and Cultural Relations. The friendship societies have nearly 1,200 branches in various republics, regions, cities, and districts; almost 30,000 work collectives at factories and institutions participate in the union's activities in the capacity of collective members.

---

* The Russian Soviet Federative Socialist Republic is the largest of the 15 constituent union republics of the Soviet Union.

About 120 organizations for friendship with the USSR are operating abroad. Undertakings which the Union of Soviet Friendship Societies carries out jointly with associations abroad and societies for friendship and cultural relations with the USSR, in which many thousands of people participate, promote mutual information and exchange of cultural values in the fields of art, literature, cinema, and education. The friendship societies are more and more actively taking part in the movement of peace-loving forces for the promotion of détente, disarmament, and a lasting peace.

Or take the Soviet Peace Fund. It was set up as a result of the patriotic initiative of working people to organize a fundraising campaign in support of the struggle of peoples for peace and national liberation. Tens of millions of Soviet citizens participate in the activities of the fund. Suffice it to say that the commissions for promoting the Soviet Peace Fund—and there are about 350 of them in the country—unite more than 4,500,000 activists in their ranks. The fund's resources come from financial contributions from voluntary work on Saturdays, money earned during "peace shifts," "peace tours," or by students who work during their vacations, from selling works of art donated to the fund, especially organized shows, concerts, lectures, sports events, and so on. In accordance with the fund's rules these donations are used for giving financial support to organizations and movements struggling for peace, national independence, and freedom; for friendship and cooperation between nations; the prohibition of all types of nuclear weapons and other means of mass destruction; and a universal and complete disarmament. At the Peace Fund's expense manufactured goods were sent to the children of Vietnam in those areas which had suffered from Chinese aggression. Help was also given in the form of food and medicines to the people of Kampuchea and the southern regions of Lebanon, as well as to Palestinian refugees who had suffered from Israeli aggression, and many other victims of social injustice.

All this is a concrete embodiment of our constitutional principle: "It is the internationalist duty of citizens of the USSR to promote friendship and cooperation with peoples of other lands and help maintain and strengthen world peace."*

---

*From the Constitution of the Soviet Union.

Looking back at the path we have traveled and evaluating the foreign policy course of the Communist Party and the Soviet state over several decades, we can say with justifiable pride that from the Soviet government's first foreign policy act, the Decree on Peace, to the Peace Program for the 1980s put forward by the Twenty-sixth Congress of the CPSU, the USSR has demonstrated the continuity of the main trends in the struggle for peace, freedom, and the security of the nations. "We have chosen the path of the struggle for peace once and for all. We shall not be led astray by imperialist provocations and threats. And we want everyone to understand: in the nuclear age peace is the most vital condition for the continuation of life on earth." These words by Leonid Brezhnev illuminate most vividly the very essence of Soviet foreign policy—its peaceableness and its humanism.

Sixty-five years have gone by since the Great October Socialist Revolution. These years have seen many, many changes in the world. Monarchies have fallen, fascist dictatorships have been overthrown and the imperialist colonial system has crumbled. The world socialist system has been born, is growing and getting stronger. Ever new countries and peoples are taking the road of socialist orientation. Imperialism is losing one position after another. And one of the main reasons for the victorious march of socialism is the fact that socialism serves as an example of the most just organization of society, guarantees genuine human rights, creates the most favorable conditions for safeguarding peace on earth and for personal development, and is, not just in words but in deeds, a society of equal opportunities for all working people.

The USSR's experience of over 60 years provides convincing proof of the fact that socialism and human rights are indivisible. As socialism is unthinkable without human rights and freedoms, so genuine human rights and freedoms are unthinkable without socialism.

As far as the campaign around the alleged "violations" of human rights in the Soviet Union and other socialist countries is concerned, its organizers have miscalculated and are walking on rather thin ice. *The State of Human Rights, USA*, a book prepared by the U.S. Communist Party, convincingly shows their pharisaism and hypocrisy. The U.S. Communists drew the correct conclusion: Capitalism is a system which arose on the basis of slave labor and many centuries of slavery, child labor, oppression of women, contempt toward those who labor and produce, the worship of masculine superiority, elitism, racism and its products—colonialism and wars of plunder—and yet this capitalism, with the help of its politicians and scribblers, dares to teach morals and human rights to the world of socialism!

The "freedoms and justice for all," as promulgated in bourgeois society, are just a dream for the overwhelming majority of the people in the capitalist countries. Leonid Brezhnev said:

> What, indeed, can the apologists of the capitalist system oppose to these real achievements of developed socialism? What real rights and freedoms are guaranteed to the masses in present-day imperialist society?
>
> The "right" of tens of millions to unemployment? Or the "right" of sick people to do without medical aid, the cost of which is enormous? Or the "right" of ethnic minorities to humiliating discrimination in employment and education, in political and everyday life? Or is it the "right" to live in perpetual fear of the omnipotent underworld of organized crime and to see how the press, cinema, TV, and radio services are going out of their way to educate the younger generation in a spirit of selfishness, cruelty and violence?

A new act of undisguised flouting of human rights, and first and foremost the right to life, was the bloody massacre of Palestinian and Lebanese civilians carried out by the Israeli military under U.S. protection in September 1982. The Beirut massacre is similar to such a Nazi atrocity as the mass murder of people at Babi Yar during the Second World War. This monstrous crime permits us to put this question bluntly: On what moral grounds exactly does the Washington administration pose as the world's defender of human rights?

Such is the true state of affairs.

It is impossible to ignore in this connection the fact that the international pacts on human rights, signed and ratified by all the countries of the socialist community, have not been recognized as yet by those who make more of a clamor than anyone about human rights.

To the Plenary Session of the CPSU Central Committee

The following is an excerpt from the Report delivered by Konstantin U. Chernenko at the Plenary Session of the CPSU Central Committee on June 14, 1983.

Comrades! I would now like to turn to the tasks with which the current international situation presents us. As you know, the United States and other NATO countries are today largely banking on achieving military superiority over the USSR and the Warsaw Treaty Organization and on the runaway arms race camouflaged by myths about the "Soviet military threat." Washington's adventuristic policy, which is whipping up international tension to the utmost, is pushing mankind toward nuclear catastrophe.

With all the complexity of international relations, the CPSU is still firmly convinced that nuclear madness can be stopped. There is no more important task for our Party than the task of safeguarding and strengthening peace. We consistently uphold the principles of peaceful coexistence and détente. The broad range of initiatives advanced recently by the Soviet Union and other countries of the socialist community shows that socialism is continuing with its peace offensive.

Statements by Yuri Andropov have a profound influence on world opinion. Their argumentation, principledness, and calm and confident tone stand in sharp contrast with the irresponsible and aggressive declarations of the White House. At the same time these statements give our class adversaries an idea of the might of our state and the futility of hoping to force the USSR into concessions which would jeopardize our security and the peaceful life of the Soviet people and the working people of the fraternal socialist countries. This position has been reiterated most forcefully in the recent statement of the Soviet government.

The major tasks of TASS, APN, the State Committee of the USSR for Television and Radio Broadcasting, and other departments concerned with foreign policy propaganda are perserveringly and convincingly to bring to the knowledge of the masses the truth about our foreign policy, to win over to its side public opinion and to expose the plans of the imperialist forces.

The class enemy openly states that it intends to wipe out the socialist system. President Reagan has announced a new "crusade" against communism. Imperialism regards "psychological warfare" as one of the main means of attaining its goal. It is being waged by the West at the highest possible, we may say, hysterical anti-Soviet and anticommunist pitch. The adversary is practicing veritable air piracy. We are faced with attempts to organize against us a full scale information and propaganda invasion and to turn radio and TV networks into tools of intervention in the internal affairs of states, tools of subversive activities.

That is why we must launch, on a large scale, offensive counter propaganda within the country as well as internationally. The Party committees must have a clear idea of what the enemy is trying to smuggle in, in what form, and through what channels, and counter these attempts promptly and effectively. . . .

The struggle of ideas on the international scene continues without respite. We will continue to wage it vigorously and with dignity, without falling for acts of provocation. The Soviet people can be confident that our Party will spare no effort in the struggle to ensure world peace and the social and national rights of the peoples.

The Ideology of Revolutionary
Creative Effort and Peace

The following are excerpts from an article by Konstantin U. Chernenko in the monthly journal Problems of Peace and Socialism* *(no. 11, November 1983). The article analyzes certain theoretical aspects of the ideological struggle in the modern world and emphasizes its interrelationship with the questions of strengthening peace on our planet.*

The strategy and tactics of the Communists' struggle in each country are in many ways determined by external conditions, above all by the balance of class forces in the international arena. That is a well-known truth. But just now there are at least three principal circumstances which, we believe, make it imperative to give special attention to this truth.

The first circumstance is the result of the almost 40-year nuclear arms race imposed by imperialism on the world. There

---

* *Problems of Peace and Socialism* is a theoretical and informational journal of the Communist and Workers' Parties, published in Prague, Czechoslovakia since 1958. It is issued monthly in 25 languages. The editorial board and the editorial staff represent nearly 50 Communist and Workers' Parties. The magazine deals with questions of Marxist-Leninist theory, the strategy and tactics of the world communist movement, the conditions of the working class, and the struggle for democracy and socialism in the developing and industrial capitalist countries. It also deals with the edification of socialism and communism in the socialist countries, problems of national liberation movements, and the internal life of the Communist and Workers' Parties. The magazine is read in 145 countries in the world, and its circulation totals one half million.

can be no winners in a nuclear war, and it cannot help to achieve any political goals. Any attempts to make use of nuclear weapons will inevitably develop into a catastrophe jeopardizing the future of life itself on the earth.

That is why the sharp aggravation of the international situation to which the aggressive policy of imperialism, U.S. imperialism above all, has now led, is a source of great alarm: it pushes mankind to the brink. To avert the fatal development of events and to ward off the war danger is a problem that is exceptionally complicated but actually soluble. The balance of sociopolitical forces and the military equilibrium which have taken shape in the international arena bear out the Communists' conclusion that a world war is not fatally inevitable, and that world peace can be maintained and strengthened on the principles of peaceful coexistence.

Consequently, the realities of the so-called nuclear age have made international conditions a determining factor in the communist movement. And, we think, also in the struggle of each party for its programmatic goals.

These considerations underlie, as is known, the CPSU's approach to international affairs. Concern for the preservation of peace on the globe has been and will continue to be in the foreseeable future the pivot of our Party's Leninist foreign policy line, the continuity of whose basic orientations was reaffirmed by the November 1982 and June 1983 Plenary Session of the CPSU-CC [Central Committee of the Communist Party of the Soviet Union]. That is also the meaning of all the concrete initiatives of the USSR in the recent period and of the broad complex of constructive proposals put forward by Yuri Andropov and designed to halt the nuclear arms race and to promote disarmament.

We are grateful to the Communist parties of the nonsocialist part of the world for their work in explaining in their countries the foreign policy positions of the CPSU and the other Marxist-Leninist parties in power. That is tangible assistance to the peoples of the socialist states carrying on a consistent struggle against nuclear war.

The myth of a "Soviet military threat," of the "excessiveness" of the Soviet Union's measures to strengthen its defense capability, of Soviet "intransigence" at the Geneva talks—all of this together with the talk about some allegedly equal responsibility of the "two superpowers" for the arms race, is being used by bourgeois propaganda not only against the USSR and its socialist allies. Anti-Sovietism has become imperialism's main ideological weapon in its fight against all those who oppose its line of unrestrained build-up of nuclear arsenals. It is on the platform of anti-Sovietism that a military coalition of the major capitalist powers is now being knocked together. By means of anti-Sovietism, imperialism tries to obtain mass support for its militaristic policy, weaken the potential of the communist movement, and split and undermine the antiwar forces as a whole. While spearheading its aggressive policy against the USSR and the socialist community as the bulwark of peace, U.S. imperialism threatens the security of all the peoples, seeks to bond them to its diktat, and ensure maximum profits for its monopolies. That is why we regard rebuffs to anti-Soviet speculations as one of the most important ideological lines in the struggle against the danger of war.

"Those who treat frivolously the defense of the country in which the proletariat has already achieved victory are the ones who destroy the connection with international socialism," said Lenin. Today, this connection is vitally necessary. It provides the indispensable prerequisite for overcoming anticommunist prejudices and preconceptions among a definite part of the working-class movement, among the political forces and social groups which, like the Communists, are acting in defense of sound principles in international relations. Their cohesion in a worldwide antiwar coalition could put up a serious obstacle in the way of a world thermonuclear war.

The second circumstance is connected with the unprecedented diversity of the problems and tasks which the Communists have to tackle in various countries and regions, something that is generated, to a considerable degree, by the uneven development of the world revolutionary process. All the more important therefore, we believe, is the collective quest for relevant forms of the Communist parties' bilateral and multilateral cooperation.

Special attention should be paid to matters of the approach to differences of opinion and disagreements which now and again arise in our movement. We believe that these cannot be a justification for weakening our international ties. That has always been true. But today it is not just true: it is one of the indispensable conditions for consolidating the political positions of each party, and of the whole of our movement, and so also for success in the struggle to preserve peace. Our Party, as the June plenary meeting stressed, considers that one of the most important tasks before it is to make an objective analysis of the substance of the difficulties and disagreements, of their root causes, and to seek ways of overcoming them on a Marxist-Leninist basis.

Imperialism seeks to weaken the communist movement precisely as an international force cemented by its common ideology and programmatic goals. Bourgeois propaganda has been trying to teach the Communists how they should arrange their relations with each other, and wants to become something of an arbiter in the discussions which are being carried on in our movement, arrogating to itself the right to judge what in it is "good" and what is "bad." Its purpose is quite obvious: it wishes the fraternal parties to fall out with each other, it, seeks to range the Communists of the socialist countries, for instance, against all the others, it wants to separate the Communist parties by their national or regional "lodgings." The attack is spearheaded against the CPSU, which is accused of trying to run the communist movement "from Moscow."

Our Party attaches tremendous importance to the explanation of its positions on these matters both at home and abroad. They are well known: the CPSU has scrupulously conducted the line of the Twenty-sixth Congress for strengthening the unity of the communist movement on the principles of Marxism-Leninism and proletarian internationalism. It sets itself the task of development with all the fraternal parties, as the resolution of the Berlin Conference of European Communist and Workers' Parties says, "internationalist, comradely, and voluntary cooperation and solidarity on the basis of the great ideas of Marx, Engels, and Lenin, strictly adhering to the principles of equality and sovereign independence of each party, noninterference in internal affairs, and respect for their free choice of different roads in the struggle for social change of a progressive nature and for socialism."

Finally, the third circumstance is that the future of mankind now largely depends on the outcome of the struggle for the hearts and minds of billions of people on the globe, as Yuri Andropov said at the June Plenary Session. Nor is there any exaggeration in putting the matter in this way.

Imperialism has always tried to back up its political offensive against the socialist world with an ideological offensive. Just now, however, we find a qualitatively new phenomenon. A veritable "psychological war," planned, financed, and directed by the governments of the imperialist countries, and coordinated on an international scale (notably within the NATO framework) is now being conducted not only against the USSR and its socialist allies, but also against the antiwar, working class and the whole revolutionary movements. As the "crusade for freedom" announced by the U.S. president some 18 months ago also testifies, this is now part and parcel of the anticommunist strategy of imperialism on a government level.

Imperialism regards its relations with the socialist world, with the working class and democratic movement, through the prism of confrontation: both in the sphere of "pure politics" and in the sphere of ideology, it equally strives to step up unrestrained tensions. In view of this, at the June Plenary Session, we considered a complex of pressing questions in the Party's propaganda and counterpropaganda work, adopted a number of concrete measures aimed to improve and extend it, and are already putting them into effect. The Plenary Session drew attention to the need to carry on ideological struggle vigorously, with dignity, and without succumbing to provocations.

I should like to emphasize the latter point. The CPSU has no intention of "playing up" to bourgeois propaganda, which, to put it mildly, is unscrupulous in the use of its means, and acts brazenly and cynically. We are resolute opponents of "psychological warfare" and have no intention of helping to fan it. But there can be no question of being passive in the ideological struggle, to say nothing of giving up our principled positions.

At the Extraordinary Plenary Session of the CPSU Central Committee

The following is an excerpt from the speech delivered by Konstantin U. Chernenko on February 13, 1984 at the Extraordinary Plenary Meeting of the Central Committee of the Communist Party of the Soviet Union, convocated soon after the death of Yuri Andropov.

. . . Drawing up plans for the further development of our country, we cannot but take into account the situation now emerging in the world. And, as you know, it is now a complicated and tense one. The correct course of the Party and the Soviet state in the sphere of foreign policy acquires even greater significance in these conditions. The struggle for lasting peace, the freedom and independence of the peoples, was always in the center of attention of Yuri Andropov. Under his direction the Political Bureau of the CPSU Central Committee and our top bodies of state authority shaped an active foreign policy which is in line with these noble principles, a policy aimed at delivering mankind from the threat of a world nuclear war. This Leninist policy of peace, the main features of which were determined at the present historical stage by the decisions of the latest congresses of the CPSU, accords with the fundamental interests of the Soviet people, and basically also of other peoples of the world. And we firmly declare: we shall not deviate an inch from that policy.

It is absolutely clear, comrades, that the success of the efforts to preserve and strengthen peace depends to a considerable degree on how great will be the influence of the socialist countries in the world arena; how vigorous, purposeful, and coordinated their actions will be. Our countries have a vital stake in peace. For the sake of this goal we will strive to broaden cooperation with all the socialist countries. By developing and deepening in every possible way cohesion and cooperation with all countries of the socialist community in all fields, including, of course, such an important one as the economic field, we are making a great contribution to the cause of peace, progress, and international security.

Addressing the fraternal countries, we say: the Soviet Union will continue to be your reliable friend and true ally.

One of the fundamentals of the foreign policy of our Party and the Soviet state has been and will remain solidarity with the peoples who have shattered the fetters of colonial dependence and embarked on the path of independent development. Especially, of course, with the peoples who have to repel the attacks of the aggressive forces of imperialism which is creating very dangerous seats of bloody violence and war conflagration in one part of the world after another. Siding with the just cause of the peoples and working for the elimination of such hotbeds is today also an essential and important direction in the struggle for lasting peace on earth. Our Party's principled stand on these issues is clear, pure, and noble. And we will unswervingly adhere to it.

Now about relations with capitalist countries. The Great Lenin bequeathed to us the principle of the peaceful coexistence of states with different social systems. We are invariably loyal to this principle. Nowadays, in the age of nuclear weapons and superaccurate missiles, the peoples need it as never before. Deplorably, some leaders of capitalist countries, to all appearances, do not clearly realize, or do not wish to realize that.

We see very well the threat which the reckless, adventurist actions of imperialism's aggressive forces are creating today for mankind, and we speak of it out loud, drawing the attention of the peoples of the whole world to that danger. We do not need any military superiority. We do not intend to dictate our will to others. But we will not let the military equilibrium that has been achieved be upset. And let no one have even the slightest doubt that we will continue to see to it that our country's defense capability is strengthened, that we have sufficient means to cool the hot heads of bellicose adventurists. This, comrades, is a very substantial prerequisite for preserving peace.

As a great socialist power the Soviet Union is fully aware of its responsibility to the peoples for preserving and strengthening peace. We are open to peaceful, mutually beneficial cooperation with states on all continents. We are for the peaceful settlement of all disputed international problems through serious, equal, and constructive talks. The USSR will in full measure cooperate with all states prepared with practical deeds to help lessen international tension and create an atmosphere of trust in the world. In other words, with those who will really pursue a policy leading not to preparing for war but to strengthening the foundations of peace. And we believe that to this end full use should be made of all the existing levers, including, of course, such a one as the United Nations Organization, which was founded precisely for preserving and strengthening peace.

Comrades, we Soviet communists are sincerely gratified that in the struggle for a peaceful future and the progress of mankind we are advancing side by side with millions of our class brothers, with numerous contingents of the world communist and working-class movement. Unswervingly loyal to the principle of proletarian internationalism, we regard with ardent sympathy and deep respect the struggle our foreign comrades are waging for the interests and rights of the working people and we see it to be our duty in every way to strengthen the bonds linking us.

This is what I would like to say today about the policy of our party in international affairs. And we are confident that the Soviet people wholeheartedly and ardently support it.

From the Speech at Yuri Andropov's Funeral

The following is an excerpt from the speech made by Konstantin U. Chernenko at the funeral of Yuri Andropov in Red Square on February 14, 1984.

An ardent champion of world peace, Yuri Vladimirovich Andropov did much to strengthen the international positions of our country and to enhance its defense potential and military capability. His thoughts and practical actions were concentrated on preserving peace and saving mankind from the threat of nuclear catastrophe. And in the present, extremely tense international situation, we clearly declare: the Soviet Union will carry on the policy of peace, of ensuring a stable and just peace for all nations, big or small.

We also reaffirm our readiness to enter into negotiations, but they must be honest negotiations based on the principle of parity and equal security. Threats cannot intimidate us. Our defense capability is strong, and we shall be able to uphold everything that has been won by the labor of the Soviet people.

To the peoples of the socialist countries we today can say again that the development of our cooperation on the basis of the tested principles of proletarian internationalism remains our invariable guide.

The Soviet Union expresses solidarity with the peoples of the newly free countries in their struggle for independence and social and economic progress and against imperialist encroachments on their freedom and genuinely democratic development.

To the Kuibyshev Constituency
in Moscow

The following is an excerpt from the March 2, 1984 speech by Konstantin U. Chernenko to the voters who nominated him as their candidate for election to the USSR Supreme Soviet in the 1984 elections.

Now let us turn to international affairs. One of the most important and imperative mandates of the Soviet electorate has been, is, and will be to cherish peace as our dearest possession and to ensure our country's security. I can tell you that the Party and the Soviet government have unswervingly followed that mandate, and they have done so in circumstances that were not easy.

You know that recent years have seen a drastic escalation of the policy of the most aggressive forces of American imperialism — a policy of undisguised militarism, striving for world supremacy, resistance to progress, and violation of the rights and freedoms of the peoples. The world has witnessed more than a few cases of that policy's practical application.

These include the invasion of Lebanon, the occupation of Grenada, the undeclared war against Nicaragua, the threats to Syria, and finally, the turning of Western Europe into a launching pad for U.S. nuclear missiles targeted on the USSR and its allies.

All this forces us to pay the gravest attention to strengthening our country's defenses. Soviet people do not want any further arms buildup; they want arms reductions on both sides. But we are bound to take care of the adequate security of our country and of our friends and allies. This is exactly what we are doing. Let everybody know that no military adventurers will ever catch us off guard and that no potential aggressor can hope to escape a crushing retaliatory strike.

At the same time, the very complexity of the current situation obliges us to double and triple our efforts in pursuing a policy of peace and international cooperation.

It is hard to name any problem important for the consolidation of peace concerning which the Soviet Union and other socialist countries have not in recent years made specific and realistic proposals. Our countries' initiatives meet with ever broader support from other countries. This was convincingly confirmed by the latest session of the UN General Assembly.

Imperialist politicians do everything possible to try to limit the international influence of the socialist countries. They try to weaken their unity and to loosen the foundations of the socialist system in those places where they think they can count on success. In these conditions it is particularly important to preserve and cement the solidarity of the fraternal socialist countries. The leaders of the Warsaw Treaty member countries once again stated their conviction on this score during their recent meeting in Moscow.

The U.S. is subjecting socialist Cuba to an economic blockade and military threats. The plans to frighten it and to force it off its chosen path, however, are doomed to failure. The guarantee of this is the unshakable will of the heroic Cuban people united round their Communist Party. Another guarantee is the solidarity of the independent countries of Latin America and of the many members of the Non Aligned Movement (NAM) with the island of freedom. The Cuban people have the strong support of the fraternal socialist countries. As regards the USSR, it has always stood and will stand by Cuba in both calm and stormy weather.

The role of socialism in international affairs could be increased, of course, by the normalization of relations with the People's Republic of China. We consistently support such a normalization. Political consultations show, however, that there are still differences on a number of questions of principle. In particular, we cannot agree to any accords damaging the interests of third countries. The exchange of opinions continues, however, and we find it useful. The Soviet Union is in favor of raising the level of these contacts to a degree acceptable to both sides.

The gradual revival of mutually beneficial contacts in the economy, culture, science, and other spheres is also useful. This does not suit those who would like to capitalize on the deterioration of relations between the USSR and China, but it benefits our two countries and helps improve the general climate in the world.

The danger of the imperialist policy of endlessly heightening tension is now obvious. The greater the threat it poses to human civilization, the greater the activity of mankind's forces of self-preservation. There is growing indignation in Western Europe at the actions of those who are sacrificing its security to the imperial ambitions of Washington. Millions of participants in the antimissile movement speak of this in no uncertain terms.

Also, far from all Western leaders and influential political parties approve of the U.S. administration's adventurism. It worries a considerable part of the American public as well. People there are realizing ever more clearly that intensified militarization and the aggravation of the international situation have not brought and will not bring the U.S. military superiority or political success. They lead only to growing criticism of Washington's bellicose course everywhere in the world. People want peace and tranquillity, not war hysteria. I can say that our talks with the leaders of the many foreign delegations that attended the funeral of Yuri Andropov confirmed this convincingly enough.

All this permits us to hope that in the end the course of events will again be turned towards the strengthening of peace, the limitation of the arms race, and the growth of international cooperation.

Détente has deep roots. One of the proofs of this is the convocation of the Stockholm conference on confidence-building measures and disarmament in Europe.*

Curbing the nuclear arms race is, of course, of key significance for peace and international security. The USSR's stand on this issue is clear. We are against rivalry in the buildup of nuclear arsenals. We have been and remain in favor of the prohibition and destruction of all types of these weapons. We have long since tabled our relevant proposals,

---

* The Conference on Confidence and Security Building Measures and Disarmament in Europe took place on January 17, 1984 in Stockholm (Sweden) with the participation of 33 European states, as well as the United States and Canada.

both at the UN and the Committee on Disarmament [in Geneva], but the United States and its allies are blocking their discussion.

As for Europe, we continue to advocate that it should be free from nuclear weapons, both medium-range and tactical. We are in favor of both sides taking the first major step in this direction without delay. In so doing the Soviet Union does not intend to strengthen its security at the expense of others, but wants equal security for all.

Unfortunately, the U.S. turned its participation in the talks on this subject into a propaganda tool to cover up the arms race and cold war policy. We have not been and shall not be a party to such a game. By deploying their missiles in Europe the Americans have created obstacles for talks not only on "European," but also on strategic nuclear weapons. The way to work out a mutually acceptable agreement lies in removing these obstacles (which would also remove the need for our countermeasures).

The U.S. administration has of late begun to issue peaceful sounding statements, calling for "dialogue."

The entire world noticed the sharp contradiction between these statements and everything that the current U.S. administration had said and, most importantly, had done and continues to do in its relations with the Soviet Union.

The assurances of its good intentions can only be taken seriously if they are backed up by deeds. Well, the Soviet Union has always been in favor of seeking mutually acceptable, practical solutions to specific questions to the benefit of both countries and the benefit of peace. There are more than a few such questions. The U.S. government has many opportunities to prove its love of peace in deed.

Why cannot the U.S. for example, ratify the treaties signed almost ten years ago with the USSR on limiting underground nuclear weapons tests, and on nuclear explosions for peaceful purposes, and complete the drawing up of an agreement on a complete and general prohibition of nuclear weapon tests? Let me remind you that the relevant talks were broken off by the United States. The U.S. can also contribute greatly to strengthening peace by agreeing to an accord on renouncing the militarization of outer space. The USSR, as is well known, has long been proposing this.

The peaceful assurances of the U.S. government would be much more credible if it accepted the proposal mutually to freeze American and Soviet nuclear arms. So much weaponry has already been accumulated that this step would not create the slightest threat to the security of either side. But it would considerably improve the general political atmosphere and, one would assume, make it easier to reach agreement on a reduction of nuclear arsenals.

To rid mankind of the possibility of the use of chemical weapons is a very important task. Talks on this subject have been going on for a long time but now the conditions necessary to resolve the issue seem to be ripening. This concerns complete and general prohibition of the use of chemical weapons, their development and production, and destruction of all the stockpiles. We are in favor of effective verification of the fulfillment of such an agreement, in favor of verification embracing the entire process of the destruction of chemical weapons, from the beginning to the very end.

It is quite possible that reaching agreement on the above issues could mark the beginning of a real change in Soviet-US relations, as well as in the whole international situation. We would welcome such a change. It is up to Washington to act now.

The policy of the powers possessing nuclear weapons is of particular importance in our time. The vital interests of all mankind and the responsibility of state leaders to the present and future generations demand that relations between these powers be subject to certain norms. In our view, these norms could be roughly as follows:

- to consider prevention of a nuclear war to be the prime aim of a state's foreign policy;
- to preclude situations likely to lead to a nuclear conflict; and should such a danger arise, to hold consultations without delay in order to prevent a nuclear conflagration;
- to renounce propaganda of nuclear war in any of its variants, either global or limited;
- to assume an obligation not to be the first to use nuclear weapons;
- under no circumstances to use nuclear weapons against non-nuclear countries which have no such weapons on their territories;
- to respect the status of the nuclear-free zone already established and to encourage the creation of new nuclear-free zones in various parts of the world;
- to prevent the proliferation of nuclear weapons in any form; not to transfer such weapons or control over them to anybody; not to deploy them on the territories of countries where there are no

such weapons; not to extend the nuclear arms race to new spheres, including outer space;

● to work step by step, on the basis of the principle of equal security, for a reduction of nuclear armaments with a view to finally destroying all types of them.

The Soviet Union has made these principles the basis of its policy. We are prepared to reach agreement with other nuclear powers at any time on jointly recognizing norms of this kind and on making them mandatory. I think that this would accord with the fundamental interests not only of the participating countries but also of the peoples of the whole world.

Interview with *Pravda*, April 1984

The following are answers given by Konstantin U. Chernenko to questions submitted by the newspaper Pravda *on April 9, 1984.*

Pravda *is a Soviet daily newspaper and the major publication of the Central Committee of the Communist Party of the Soviet Union. Founded in 1912 by Vladimir Ilyich Lenin, the paper has a circulation of over 10 million copies.*

Q: What is your assessment of the situation in the world at the present moment? In particular, are there any signs of a change for the better in the policy of the United States of America?

A: Regrettably, the situation in the world is not improving. It remains very dangerous, and this is due to the U.S. administration's continued reliance on military force, on a policy of seeking military superiority and imposing its ways on other peoples. This was confirmed once again by President Reagan's recent speech at Georgetown University.

Even if peace rhetoric is sometimes heard from Washington, it is impossible, however hard one tries, to discern behind it any signs whatsoever of a readiness to back up words with deeds. To put it another way, new words do not mean a new policy.

Let us turn to such a cardinal issue as ending the nuclear arms race.

Perhaps the people in the White House have realized the danger and lack of prospect of this race and begun to show restraint? Nothing of the sort. On the contrary, in the United States more and more new programs for developing and deploying nuclear weapons are being pushed through. The deployment of U.S. nuclear missiles in Western Europe is continuing as well. All this is being done to disrupt in one way or another the existing balance of forces.

Such actions are wholly incompatible with the task of ending the arms race. And it is not at all by chance that the United States has deliberately undermined the very process of limiting and reducing nuclear arms and wrecked the talks both on strategic arms and on nuclear arms in Europe.

Our contacts with the American side also show that no positive changes have taken place in the position of the United States on these cardinal issues.

While persisting in its former line, a line which has brought about the collapse of the Geneva talks, and continuing to deploy its missiles in Western Europe, Washington holds forth about its readiness for a resumption of the talks. But, one may ask, talks on what? On how many and specifically what type of missiles targeted on the Soviet Union and our allies the United States can deploy in Europe? Such talks are not for us.

There is no need to convince us of the usefulness of dialogue, the usefulness of talks. The moment the United States and the other NATO countries, which are acting at one with it, take steps to restore the situation that existed before the deployment of the new U.S. missiles in Western Europe, the Soviet Union will readily respond. Such is the real road to talks.

Q: What is the situation in the other areas of arms limitation and disarmament?

A: Progress on the other issues is also being blocked by the United States. I shall dwell on two or three of them.

First of all, space. This is not the first year that the Soviet Union has been pressing for an agreement on preventing the arms race from spreading to outer space. We have been constantly raising this issue with leaders of the United States. We do this because we clearly realize the dire consequences that the militarization of outer space entails.

Meanwhile, the U.S. president has officially informed the United States Congress, a few days ago, that the U.S. government is beginning to carry out a broad arms build-up program in space and has no intention of reaching agreement with the Soviet Union on preventing the militarization of space supposedly because of the difficulties of verification.

They quite bluntly and frankly do not want to negotiate. But making a mockery of common sense they express a readiness to talk with us with the sole purpose of agreeing that accord on this issue is impossible. This is how the people in Washington understand political dialogue and negotiations in general.

Let us take another key issue—the banning of chemical weapons.

As early as 1972 the USSR and other socialist countries proposed at the Geneva Disarmament Committee the conclusion of a convention on the prohibition of the development, production, and stockpiling of chemical weapons and on their destruction. They then submitted a draft of such a convention.

Since then we have returned to this matter on many occasions, specifying our proposals and making them more detailed. But all these years the United States has impeded the conclusion of a convention on the total prohibition of chemical weapons. It has simply engaged in obstruction.

Now they in Washington have decided to pose as the champions of a ban on chemical weapons. For several months now the U.S. leaders have been promising to table in Geneva some proposals on this score. But promises are only promises and nothing is known at all as to what they will lead to; meanwhile, as it follows from the president's remarks, a program of building up and modernizing chemical weapons, which are to be stationed both on U.S. territory and beyond it, is being stepped up in the United States.

Here is yet another example. Two Soviet-American treaties on limiting underground nuclear explosions have not been put into effect so far. They were signed almost ten years ago and we have proposed many times that the United States should ratify them. However, to this day it has refused to do so.

The subterfuges that have been resorted to in this! At first it was said that ratification of these treaties would hinder talks on the universal and complete prohibition of nuclear weapon tests. Then, when these talks too were broken off, references began to be made to difficulties of verification.

Of course, the issue here has nothing to do with verification, as the treaties that have been signed contain most thoroughly worked out provisions on this score. The matter lies in something else—in Washington's refusal to bind its hands with any limitations whatsoever that would impede the buildup and perfection of nuclear arms.

I have touched on the question of verification also because the United States makes recourse to it whenever it does not want an agreement. When there has been a real desire to reach agreement on measures for arms reduction and disarmament, verification has not been, nor can it be, an obstacle. This is borne out by past experience.

Incidentally, considering the policy and practices of the United States, we are no less interested, but probably more so than the United States, in reliable verification, in adequate and specific measures on arms limitation and disarmament.

Q: It is sometimes said in the West that the Soviet Union does not wish to reach agreement with the United States now because the USSR is waiting for the outcome of the presidential election there. Would you comment on this?

A: I will say this. Those who spread such ideas either do not know or, most probably, deliberately distort our policy. It is a principled policy and is not subject to transient considerations.

In the course of development of Soviet-American relations we have dealt with different administrations in Washington. In those cases where realism and a responsible approach to relations with the Soviet Union were shown by U.S. leaders, it can be said that things proceeded normally. This also had a favorable effect on the general situation in the world. In the absence of such a realistic approach our relations worsened accordingly.

Today too we are for having normal, stable relations with the United States, relations based on equality, equal security, and noninterference in each other's internal affairs.

Insinuations about "calculations" on our part in connection with the forthcoming election in the United States, it seems, are an attempt by some people to conceal their own reluctance to negotiate with the Soviet Union on questions that need to be settled. As to the state of affairs in this respect, one can have an idea of it by comparing the positions of the two sides even on the issues that I have just mentioned.

Q: What in you opinion should be done so that people can stop living in a state of constant anxiety about peace?

A: First and foremost, it is essential that the policy of states, especially of states possessing nuclear weapons, be aimed at eliminating the war danger, at consolidating peace.

Efforts should be directed first of all at stopping and reversing the arms race. It is time to go over from general discussion about the usefulness of talks to eliminating the serious obstacles that have been place in the path of the limitation and reduction of armaments, of the development of trust and mutually advantageous cooperation.

I have already mentioned several far-reaching proposals put forward by the Soviet Union concerning specific issues in these areas. There are also other major questions that require concentrated and concerted efforts.

There is no doubt that a decisive turn for the better in the world would be facilitated by a commitment by all nuclear states not to be the first to use nuclear weapons and to impose a quantitative and qualitative freeze on nuclear arsenals. This does not require complicated negotiations. Political resolve is what is needed here. The result would no doubt be of immense significance in every respect. The main thing is that there would be a clear demonstration of a readiness to give up attempts to achieve military superiority over others. Our country does not seek such superiority, but neither will it allow such superiority over it.

It is extremely important in general that certain norms of conduct promoting peace should be introduced in relations between states possessing nuclear arms. I have spoken on this in detail before.

The task of creating an atmosphere of trust in international relations is an urgent one. This calls for a responsible and balanced policy on the part of all states and the adoption of relevant practical measures in this direction. A combination of major steps of a political nature and having the force of international law with measures in the field of military technology as proposed by the Soviet Union and the other socialist countries, would make success at the Stockholm Conference possible, and make its results a major contribution to the strengthening of European and international security.

The most vigorous efforts should be made to eliminate existing seats of tension and military conflicts in various parts of the world and to prevent the appearance of new ones.

In other words, there are many possibilities for promoting by concrete deeds the consolidating of peace and international security.

The Soviet Union is prepared to cooperate with all states in the attainment of these aims.

Reply to an Appeal by American Scientists

Prominent U.S. scientists Richard L. Garwin and Carl Sagan sent a letter to the General Secretary of the Communist Party of the Soviet Union, Chairman of the Presidium of the Supreme Soviet of the USSR, Konstantin U. Chernenko. In the letter they expressed deep concern over the menace of militarizing space. They also shared their views on the limitations of manned spaced ships used for military purposes.

The following is the response of Konstantin Chernenko, issued on May 19, 1984.

The appeal you made to the leaders of the countries of the world not to allow lethal weapons to find their way into space and to prevent the emergence of a new area of the arms race is extremely timely and important. We thoroughly understand the concern being voiced by prominent American scientists in this connection.

The cosmos has become a symbol of the grand achievements of science and technology. The peaceful uses of space yield no small return. However, there are some who would like to turn space into an arena of war and aggression. As is clear from the plans announced in the United States, it is projected to deploy antimissile systems in space, to make room for the operation of different kinds of antisatellite systems, and to station the new types of super weapons devised to strike at targets on the land, in the air, and at sea.

The Soviet Union is resolutely opposed to competing in the race in any arms, space arms included. At the same time it should be clear that, faced with a threat from outer space, the Soviet Union would be compelled to take measures for reliably ensuring its security. The plans to blaze a trail to military superiority through outer space are based on illusions. However, there appears to be no desire to give up such plans, and this is fraught with extremely dangerous consequences. Preventing events from taking such a course before it is too late is the duty of responsible statesmen, scientists, and all who are truly concerned about the future of humankind.

The Soviet Union reaffirms that it is ready to do its utmost to prevent the sinister plans for taking the arms into outer space from becoming a reality. It is our conviction that a policy aimed at reliably protecting outer space from the deployment of weapons there should become an obligatory norm of conduct of countries and a universally recognized international requirement.

We are decidedly against the development of large-scale antimissile defense systems, which cannot be regarded otherwise than designed for carrying out nuclear aggression with impunity. A treaty that bans the creation of such systems does exist—the Soviet-American treaty of unlimited duration on antiballistic missile systems. It should be strictly observed. A solemn renunciation of the very idea of deploying antimissile systems in outer space would accord with the spirit and letter of the treaty and with the task of ensuring the peaceful status of outer space in the interests of all humankind. Such a step would be regarded everywhere in the world as a manifestation of genuine concern for the peaceful future of humankind.

The question of banning antisatellite weapons also cannot tolerate delay. The deployment of such weapons would lead to an abrupt destabilization of the situation and to an increase in the threat of an unexpected attack, and it would undermine efforts to ensure trust between nuclear nations. You as scientists understand better than anyone else how dangerous all of this is.

Urgent steps are necessary before the menacing process of militarizing outer space becomes irreversible. In this question there should be no room for propagandistic tricks or for attempts at ensuring temporary advantages for oneself. Preventing outer space from being militarized is a problem that is important to all humankind. It requires thorough solutions. Such solutions are quite feasible. It is essential to realize one's total responsibility to the peoples and to show desire for accord.

In our attempts to block the way of weapons into outer space, we have suggested coming to terms about banning the use of force in outer space and from space with respect to Earth. This accord would also presuppose, in particular, full renunciation of antisatellite weapons, including the destruction of already existing systems. In order to make it easier to reach agreement, the Soviet Union has unilaterally announced a moratorium on putting antisatellite weapons in outer space as long as other countries act in the same way.

The Soviet initiative has met with wide support in the world. There is no justification and there cannot be any justification for refusing to begin working out appropriate practical measures. What is required is to start official talks without any conditions or reservations with a view to reliably cutting off all channels of militarization of outer space. It is the duty of the political and public figures of every country to promote this just and profoundly humane goal. The Soviet Union is fully determined to do everything it can for an appropriate understanding to be reached.

As far as your specific consideration is concerned, the one pertaining to the provision of the Soviet draft treaty on restrictions on the military use of both manned and unmanned spacecraft, it could be discussed during official talks.

Let me take this opportunity to wish you success in your lofty activities to prevent the spreading of the arms race to outer space.

Message to the U.S.–USSR Trade and Economic Council

The following is the text of a message of greetings sent by Konstantin U. Chernenko on May 23, 1984 to the participants of the eighth annual meeting of the U.S.–USSR Trade and Economic Council, held this year in Washington, D.C.

I greet the participants of the eighth annual meeting of the U.S.–USSR Trade and Economic Council.

The Council, which was formed more than ten years ago, plays a positive role in the development of cooperation between the business circles of our two countries. Your meeting reaffirms mutual interest in such cooperation.

The Soviet Union consistently advocates stable, broad, trade and economic links with all countries, including, of course, the United States—on the basis of the principles of equality and mutual benefit without any discrimination. We are convinced that such an approach to trade, which traditionally serves as an active means of communication among nations, is important also from the viewpoint of establishing necessary mutual understanding and building up confidence. This is of special significance under present-day conditions.

I wish the participants in the work of the Council successes in their useful activities.

Reply to Joseph Kingsbury-Smith

The following are answers given by Konstantin U. Chernenko on June 11, 1984 to questions addressed to him by the well-known U.S. journalist, Joseph Kingsbury-Smith.

Q: During the debate on the Reagan Administration's military programs, which it is planning to finance from the defense budget for the 1985 fiscal year, the House of Representatives of the U.S. Congress voted for an amendment prohibiting appropriations for the holding of tests of U.S. antisatellite weapons in space if the USSR and other countries abstain from holding such tests. In light of the above voting, would the USSR Government agree, on a basis of reciprocity with the United States, to freeze antisatellite weapons tests for yet another year or more?

A: It is evident that the voting in the House of Representatives reflects the concern of the U.S. legislators over the possibility of the arms race spreading to outer space. There is every reason for such disquiet. The question now is this: either the militarization of space will be prevented or else it will become the source of a formidable danger suspended over all humankind.

As regards the Soviet Union, it has consistently advocated outer space remaining peaceful. Striving to contribute to resolving the task, the USSR last year had already assumed a unilateral commitment not to put antisatellite weapons in space, introducing, in other words, a unilateral moratorium on such launchings for as long as other states, including the

U.S., keep abstaining from placing antisatellite weapons of any type in space. It goes without saying that the commitment also covers tests launchings of antisatellite weapons.

This moratorium announced by the Soviet Union continues in operation. At the same time, with all its usefulness, we regard the moratorium only as a first step toward the total prohibition of antisatellite weapons, including the liquidation of such systems already in existence. It is precisely for this reason that we propose to the United States to embark without delay on official talks with a view toward achieving an agreement to this effect.

The Soviet Union's specific proposals on this question are well-known; they enjoy the support of an overwhelming majority of the UN member-states. Only the U.S. Government is against them.

Q: Could a freeze on antisatellite weapons tests be effectively verified. And if yes, then how?

A: The Soviet Union is convinced that a freeze on antisatellite-weapons tests can be verified, and highly reliably at that, first and foremost by the national technical means available to the sides. Statements by many prominent U.S. experts also speak in favor of such a conclusion.

Effective verification of the observance by the sides of a moratorium with respect to orbital antisatellite weapons could be ensured by the space tracking means possessed by the sides. As for suborbital antisatellite systems, one could, in addition to those already mentioned, make use of other radioelectronic means belonging to the United States and the Soviet Union, deployed on land, in the world ocean, and in space. In unclear situations exchanges of information and consultations could be carried out. Should the need arise, other forms can also be found.

Given a real interest in finding effective solutions, any related issues, including those of verification, could be successfully resolved in the course of the talks proposed by the Soviet Union, both on the antisatellite weapons and on the prevention of militarization of space in general.

I would wish to re-emphasize this: agreement on these questions must be sought without delay while space weapons have not yet been deployed and while a breakthrough in the space weapons race, unpredictable in its possible consequences, has not yet been made. Tomorrow it may be too late.

Those who attempt, by prematurely invoking the "impossibility" of verifying agreements limiting an arms race in space, to rule out any productive talks in this field are consciously bent on being free to pursue the course of space militarization in the hope of gaining military advantages.

I shall put it bluntly: this course has no prospect of succeeding and is dangerous. If it should ever lead anywhere, it is only to a steep escalation of the war threat. This cannot be allowed to happen. The need is for urgent and effective measures to keep outer space peaceful. The Soviet Union is unreservedly in favor of this road.

Interview with *Pravda*, June 1984

The following are answers given by Konstantin U. Chernenko on June 13, 1984 to questions submitted by the newspaper Pravda.

Q: Recently the leaders of seven major Western states held a meeting in London. What, in your opinion, determined the nature and the contents of that meeting?

A: The regular meeting of the "Seven" was purportedly convened to examine economic issues. Above all, however, it concerned politics. This is clearly indicated by the documents adopted in London.

Again, as was also the case at the NATO session in May, much was said to declare peaceable intentions and an interest in reducing the level of armaments, including nuclear armaments. Again the Soviet Union was urged to engage in a dialogue and talks. Regrettably, however, these intentions and appeals failed to be backed up with anything tangible. Why is this happening?

One explanation lies right on the surface; the American press literally hums about it. There are considerations connected with the presidential elections in the United States.

The more important reason is that the participants in the meeting of the "Seven" rubberstamped provisions that run counter to the interests of détente, disarmament, and peace. The dialogue and talks are mentioned since they need a screen to somehow cover up the transformation of the territories of some of the Western European countries into launching pads for the new U.S. missiles. Reality, however, is that the line for missile deployment remains unshakable, which has been repeatedly stated by the U.S. Administration. Washington and other NATO capitals, are, of course, aware of the fact that this is increasingly blocking the possibility of talks, raising still higher the barrier in the way of reducing the level of nuclear armaments. To aim new U.S. nuclear missiles at the Soviet Union and its allies and at the same time to urge talks— is this not political duplicity?

Is there a need for a dialogue and for talks? Both yesterday and today our answer has been the same—yes. But a dialogue that is honest, and talks that are serious. We stand ready to engage in these at any time.

The Soviet Union has put forward proposals for deep cuts in nuclear armaments; their realization would not infringe on anyone's interests. We advocate that these issues be considered in earnest at the negotiating table as soon as the U.S. side withdraws its essentially peremptory conditions for talks. If this were to happen, any real, positive shift in the stance of the United States and its allies would not be left without a proper response on our part.

The Soviet Union suggests reaching accords on a whole package of measures capable of really reducing the level of military confrontation and precluding the use and threat of force in international life. These proposals are known.

I will single out, as an example, the problem of preventing the militarization of outer space. The entire world recognizes its utmost importance. Our proposals on how to resolve this problem have been submitted to Washington. But it does not want to handle this problem, does not want even to discuss it. In all likelihood, the U.S. Administration is fond only of its own ambitious stance, which is opening outer space to the most formidable kinds of armaments and is thus trying to gain military superiority. It is clear that in this very important sphere, too, we do not see a reciprocal desire for solid talks, never mind any effort toward an agreement. No talk about the benefit of dialogue will camouflage this fact.

We address our unequivocal appeal to the United States and its allies: it is high time they confirmed by real actions their share of responsibility for the destiny of peace, realized the futility of the position-of-strength policy and reliance on the arms race, and displayed a genuine, rather than apparent, readiness for dialogue and for talks in order to find mutually acceptable solutions to questions on which the future of humankind depends. The Soviet Union is not wanting in such readiness.

Q: How can the placing of the issues of "international terrorism" at the London conference be appraised?

A: In London this problem was turned inside out. They discussed some technical details, but ignored the main thing. And they did that deliberately.

Criminal acts of terrorism are being committed in front of the whole world, committed on a small scale, on a medium scale, and on a large scale, single-handedly and by groups or even directly with the broad involvement of the armed forces of some states. This was the case in Grenada, this was the case in Lebanon, this is the case now in Nicaragua. But for some reason they did not mention a word about all this at the London conference. Apparently, they decided that if they played it false, they would play it loud.

The Soviet Union has condemned and condemns now any manifestations of terrorism. And we resolutely reject the policy of the United States, which has opted for terrorism as a method of conducting affairs with other states and peoples.

And it does not befit those who practice "state terrorism" to set forth declarations on "democratic values," as was done at the London conference. This is just a reinterpretation of the adventurist concept of the "crusade," another attempt to transfer ideological struggle to the sphere of interstate relations.

On the whole, the statements issued both on terrorism and on "democracy" serve the aims of pulling major capitalist states, including Japan, even closer to the militarist course of the U.S. Administration.

Q: And how can the discussion of international economic problems in London be summed up?

A: A lengthy declaration was adopted on this theme. It contains many words, but they drown out the acute socio-economic problems that are intrinsic to the capitalist system in general and that have become even more painful of late. This includes, first of all, unemployment, inflation and the soaring cost of living; that is, all those phenomena that mercilessly hit the broad masses of working people in capitalist countries. No serious measures to take the sting out of these problems were outlined in London. But, then, how could they have been if it was the U.S. recipe of letting the rich become richer and the poor poorer that was being forced on the meeting?

One can also feel that, in exerting massive pressure on its partners, Washington is trying to resolve its own economic problems and difficulties at the expense of others. The trade and economic expansion of Japan is also making itself felt. In short, the knot of interimperialist contradictions is being tightened still further, and they come to the surface one way or another.

The economic problems would be a hundred times easier to solve if it were not for the arms race—this insatiable machine gobbling up countless intellectual and material resources. But it was precisely this central issue that was ignored at the meeting of the "Seven."

It is indicative that the problems of profound concern to the developing countries also found themselves shoved to the back burner. Declaratory statements of a general nature cannot hide the fact that there is ruthless exploitation of the economically weak countries of Africa, Asia, and Latin America by the industrially developed capitalist countries, above all the United States. Judging by everything, the intention is to continue this policy. This can lead to only one result—the deepening of the chasm between the rich and the poor countries, which will make tomorrow even more difficult than today. Here too, the arms race that is being spurred on by Washington and its NATO allies is making itself felt in the most immediate manner.

It is no coincidence that everywhere around the world the question is now being asked as to whether the London meeting set any goals of assisting in any way in improving the situation in the developing countries. The answer given to this question in the developing countries themselves is clearly in the negative.

In light of what took place at the meeting of the "Seven," it would, apparently, not be unwarranted to remember the position of the Soviet Union and the socialist countries, which consistently advocate restructuring international economic relations on an equitable and democratic basis. This has just been confirmed with renewed force by the CMEA summit meeting now in session in Moscow. Our indefatigable and, one can say without exaggeration, energetic struggle for halting the arms race aims, in addition to its immediate objective—

that of reducing the military threat—at reconverting the huge material means to be released to the goals of improving the well-being of the peoples, to the needs of health care, culture, education, and housing construction. A significant part of the means thus released could be used as assistance to the peoples of the developing countries. We are pursuing this line in our bilateral relations, and we advocate it at international forums, including the United Nations. We shall continue to be guided by this in the future, too.

Reply to Sean MacBride

Sean MacBride, a prominent Irish public figure, winner of the Lenin and Nobel Peace Prizes and chairman of the International Peace Bureau, sent a letter recently to Konstantin U. Chernenko. In the letter, he expressed a number of ideas concerning the development of relations between the USSR and the United States so that general and complete disarmament is eventually achieved. Konstantin Chernenko replied on August 11, 1984 in the following letter.

———————————

Your message, expressing your intention to promote the attainment of general and complete disarmament, is consonant with sentiments that are now widespread throughout the world. It is obvious to every thinking person that a further buildup of nuclear arms and, even more so, the endeavors to spread the arms race to outer space, confront humanity with the threat of an all-out nuclear catastrophe.

You write that the latest statements by the U.S. president about the senselessness of a nuclear war and about the need to rid the Earth of nuclear weapons ostensibly open up an opportunity for serious negotiations. As you well know, a good deal of words about peace and negotiations have already been uttered from the U.S. side. However, all practical actions by the U.S. Administration are at variance with their proclaimed striving for talks, for improving relations. It is clear that this by no means signifies a change in the present U.S. stand.

We, for our part, have stated more than once that we would like to have good relations with the United States. But both sides should display the proper attitude in this matter. I think that your conclusion, prompted by your wide political and life experience, that the sincere good intentions of the sides and appropriate preparations should be the indispensable and really solid foundation of any talks between the USSR and the United States is correct. We also adhere to this point of view.

The Soviet leadership believes that concrete actions, and not words, by the U.S. Administration can unblock the way to normalizing the atmosphere in our relations with the United States.

With best wishes for your health and success in your noble activities in the name of peace among the peoples.

Interview with *Pravda*, September 1984

The following are answers given by Konstantin U. Chernenko on September 1, 1984 to questions submitted by Pravda.

Q: The American Administration has recently set forth once again in concentrated form its foreign policy priorities. What can you say about this?

A: Indeed, U.S. leaders have delivered many speeches lately, especially in connection with the Republican Party's convention. These statements and the election platform adopted at the convention allow one to make judgments about the present American Administration's view of the world and about its current intentions. One should say that all this leaves a depressing impression.

Political priorities and, what is more important, practical actions by those who shape U.S. foreign policy are apparently oriented toward the further dangerous heightening of international tension. Many political and public circles also share this judgment.

In Washington they are flaunting with open cynicism their great-power ambitions and exaggerated notions about America's role and place in the modern world. They claim the role of being the strongest, of ruling the destinies of peoples and dictating their will to everyone everywhere. In short, they are now talking about a "crusade" not only against socialism, but against the entire world.

At a time when people feel concern over the future, when they expect from their governments a highly responsible policy aimed at consolidating international peace, at radically limiting and terminating the arms race and at eliminating seats of conflict, they in Washington proclaim their intention to act with the help of raw military force.

Obsessed by force, they are simply losing a sense of reality. The world has drastically changed. Force cannot resolve its problems. This has been proved more than once, including the experience of the United States of America itself. It is impossible to consolidate one's security at the expense of the security of others. The calculations to gain military superiority in the hope of winning a nuclear war are just as unrealistic today. I am repeating: The Soviet Union is not seeking military superiority over others, but it will not allow superiority over itself. Probably, some people in the United States still find it hard to put up with this, but one will have to reckon with the fact that our two states may deal with each other only on an equal footing, on the basis of consideration for the legitimate interests of each other. There is no sensible alternative to this.

Attempts are being made in Washington to justify the position-of-strength policy by some ''moral'' considerations. They would like to assume the right to determine which states are ''democracies'' and which are not, who should be described as advocates of ''freedom''—like the Pinochet regime in Chile and racists in South Africa—and who should become a target of large-caliber guns, like in Lebanon and elsewhere. In other words, everything which they regard as permissible for themselves, up to ousting legitimate governments, conducting a policy of state-sponsored terrorism and waging undeclared wars, is proclaimed moral. Here lies the main cause of the aggravation of the existing and emergence of new seats of tension, be it in the Middle East, southern Africa, Central America or other regions.

We are thoroughly convinced that conflict stituations can and should be settled only by peaceful means, with full consideration for the interests of those directly concerned, guided by the broad objectives of strengthening international security.

About the Middle East. Tragic events that are taking place there show that peace cannot be achieved through separate deals and, even more so, through military interference. The situation in that region can be radically improved only through collective efforts by all parties concerned. On this premise rests the Soviet plan for a Middle East peace settlement, which has received broad support in the Arab world, and not only there.

Summing up, I would like to stress: hard as the United States might flex its military muscle, it will not manage to alter the world. The world will not live according to American standards.

What is necessary is a transition to a policy of realism, common sense and businesslike cooperation in handling tasks that are facing humanity.

Q: In Washington they are continuing to declare their readiness for talks with the Soviet Union on outer space. What are, in your opinion, the real prospects of holding talks on the prevention of space militarization?

A: They in Washington do not mind talking about their readiness for talks and have even announced their intention to send a delegation to Vienna. As a matter of fact, the U.S. Administration does not want to resolve the problem of preventing the militarization of outer space—its aspirations are directed at concealing its negative stand from the world public, and at justifying the elaboration and realization of space armaments plans.

That is why our proposal for holding talks on outer space has not received a positive response from the American side. During a discussion of the objectives of the talks, it tried, first of all, to change the very subject of negotiations. Instead of arranging the discussion of the specific issue of prohibiting space weapons, the United States started to insist on considering questions dealing with nuclear armaments in general, in other words, the questions discussed at the Geneva talks that had been broken off as a result of known U.S. actions.

What subject does the Soviet Union propose to discuss at the talks? The subject is how to preclude the spread of the arms race into outer space and fully renounce space strike systems, including antisatellite weapons. In other words, the aim is to prevent a war threat to Earth from outer space, and to outer space from Earth and from space itself. As the first step, we propose that a reciprocal moratorium be imposed on the testing and deployment of space strike systems simultaneously with the beginning of the negotiations.

Such an agreement would not only prevent the arms race in outer space, but, what is no less important, would facilitate the solution of questions of limiting and reducing other strategic armaments. I would like to emphasize that.

The problem of space armaments cannot be resolved by half or by one quarter. It is impossible, for instance, to ban one type of antisatellite weapon and allow another, or ban only antisatellite weapons and give the green light, so to say, to other types of space weaponry.

In both instances, the point at issue is the same race in space armaments. The U.S. stand, in fact, comes down to the desire to legalize a race of this kind. This follows from official statements by American leaders, made either in public or during contacts they had with us.

Thus, the American side's approach to the problem of outer space and, correspondingly, to the aims of the talks is directly opposite to our approach. What then would be the sense of holding the talks? Talks are needed not for the sake of talks, but for reaching accords that would effectively prevent the race in space armaments.

One would like to hope that the realization of the need to adopt joint measures to prevent space militarization will ultimately prevail in the ruling circles of the United States.

Q: It is hoped in the political circles of many countries that a Soviet-American dialogue will be resumed. What is your attitude to the dialogue, to talks in the present conditions?

A: As I understand, what is meant is a dialogue and talks on major political issues—on questions whose solution determines the fate of the world. I have already said: there is no need to convince us of the benefit of this dialogue.

We have always favored serious and concrete talks. We approach from these positions to search for the solution of the existing issues with the present U.S. Administration, too. Regrettably, we have encountered a different attitude to negotiations. Let us take such an issue of major importance as the limitation and reduction of nuclear armaments—both strategic and intermediate-range. For more than a year Washington looked for any pretexts not to get involved in the talks at all. This time was used for something else—to get new large-scale military programs under way.

When the talks in Geneva started, it soon became clear that U.S. representatives came there not with constructive objectives, but with intentions to secure solutions that would give the United States military advantages over the Soviet Union. There is, of course, no sense in such talks.

It is only with the strict observance of the principle of equality and equal security of the sides that serious and productive talks become possible. Washington's renunciation of this principle resulted in the collapse of the Geneva talks. It is Washington which undermined these talks.

Today enough issues remain which need discussion and solution, and we will have to handle them.

I want to reaffirm with all certainty our readiness for dialogue, for honest and serious talks aimed at finding accords that take into account the security interests of all countries and peoples.

Such is our understanding of dialogue.

About the Editor

Victor Pribytkov, born in 1935, is an assistant to the General Secretary of the Central Committee of the Communist Party of the Soviet Union, Konstantin U. Chernenko, and is a deputy to the USSR Supreme Soviet.

A lawyer by education, he has a long record of service in Communist Party organizations. He is also an experienced journalist, a member of the USSR Union of Journalists, and the author of many publications about the ideological struggle and communist edification.